Integrating Work and Family Life

THE HOME-WORKING FAMILY

Betty Beach

State University
of New York
Press

Published by
State University of New York Press, Albany

© 1989 State University of New York

For information, address State University of New York
Press, State University Plaza, Albany, NY 12246

Library of Congress Cataloging-in Publication Data

Beach, Betty, 1947–
      Integrating work and family life : the home-working family / Betty
   Beach
         p.   cm.
      Bibliography: p.
      Includes index.
      ISBN 0–7914–0004–2.   ISBN 0–7914–0005–0 (pbk.)
      1. Work and family.   2. Home-based business.   I. Title.
   HD4904.25.B4 1989
   306'.36—dc19   88–26169
                                                                         CIP

10   9   8   7   6   5   4   3   2   1

Contents

Preface

One of the hottest topics of the 1980s among family researchers has been the interaction between work and family life. Propelled by the dramatic changes created by women's entry into the work world, social scientists have delved into the complex knot entangling work and family lives, turning away from their earlier preoccupation with work and family as separate entities. As women, and more particularly, married women with children, move out of the home into the workplace, major dislocations in our social conceptions of gender, parenthood, and work identity have occurred. Work life and family life no longer remain separate, inviolate, and gender-specific, neatly divisible into distinct social realms, as researchers in earlier decades perceived them. Instead, undeniable connections exist between work and family life, connections often revealing confusion, competition, and exhaustion for the individuals involved.

Family researchers, busily identifying sources of work-family tension, locate them variously in intrafamily dynamics (such as unequal sharing of household responsibilities), in workplace structures (such as rigid time schedules) and in the larger socioeconomic structure (such as capitalism as a patriarchal system). Numerous studies highlight time conflicts, child care cost and availability, and exhausting multiple role demands as particularly daunting to families seeking to place work and family life in a more harmonious balance. The proliferation of work-family research over the past decade underscores the difficulty of balancing these two domains as it reveals ever more obstacles exacting a heavy personal and family cost.

The ease with which researchers identify impediments to balancing reflects both a social reality and a predisposition to consider work as the more powerful social influence. How work influences family life represents a second wave of social science research, following the dominant first wave which emphasized the separateness of these spheres. Accordingly, most research of recent years concentrated on how dominant work demands intruded on family life. Investigators studied work spillover into family life, looking at how work schedules, job demands, and the emotional effects of working forced families to bend and accommodate. While theoretically positing that effects could be mutual, such research heavily emphasized the unidirectionality of the work realm's influence on family life.

An emerging third wave in work-family research, conceptualized as an interactive model, aims to identify more specifically how work and family mutually interact and influence each other (Chow and Berheide 1988). This developing model "recognizes the mutual interdependence between family and work, taking into account the reciprocal influences of work and family and acknowledging their independent as well as joint effects, directly and indirectly, on the psychological state and social conditions of individuals" (Chow and Berheide 1988, 25). This model examines specific occupational and family circumstances which affect how work and family life connect with each other.

The study of home-working families reported in this book fits into this interactive model. Although working at home is the focus of considerable public policy controversy, this book is not an examination of the pros and cons of home work per se. Rather, the focus here is on how families use home work as a strategy for integrating work and family lives. It explores how fifteen rural families use home work, concentrating on their experiences in order to build an understanding of the very specific conditions under which these two roles intersect. Most academic writing on home work is negative, condemning it as an exploitive strategy built on women's inequality in the social and economic world (Boris 1985, 1987). I cover some of these perspectives in the second chapter, but align the contents of the book with those seeking to understand how work and family interact on a microsocial

level rather than with those seeking to make blanket condemnations or advocacy of home work as a tool of public policy.

My interest in home work as a family work strategy was
initially piqued as an early childhood educator. I came to re-
alize that several children in my nursery school groups displayed quite concrete knowledge of their parent's work, a
knowledge generated by their opportunity to participate in parental work when it occurred in the home. As a resident of a
rural community, I recognized that working at home is a common alternative utilized by many families in non-urban economies. Aware of their existence and interested in children's
input into the work-family equation, I thought that studying
work-at-home families would provide a natural laboratory for
examining the interaction of work and family life. Shared
work and family space appeared to promise abundant opportunities to learn about this interaction and the specific consequences flowing from such a work arrangement. Thus, my
intent was always a microfocus, a deliberate sifting of the specific circumstances affecting the outcome in this particular
work-family interface.

Although little precedent exists for an intensive scrutiny
of home-working families' lives, several concepts from social
science provided guideposts. Especially helpful were the ideas
of "permeability" offered by Piotrkowski (1978) and "absorptiveness" set forth by Kanter (1977). Simply put, permeability
refers to the degree of access between work and family realms.
For most working families, home and workplace are physically
distinct and relatively inaccessible. From such a physical and
consequent psychological barrier emanate many of the reported incompatibilities between work and family. Home-
working families, however, presumably join work and family
space in some degree; the task was to explore this degree and
describe how it affected family life. The second concept, absorptiveness, measures the degree to which not only is the
worker involved in his/her work but the family may be drawn
in as well, "Occupational pursuits . . . which also implicate
other family members and command their direct participation in the work system in either its formal or informal
aspects" (Kanter 1977, 26). Specifically, Kanter goes on to
suggest that "co-extensive home-workplaces" may be one
characteristic of absorptiveness, and that "there is an impor-

tant research task to be performed in simply documenting the extent of such coextensive home-workplaces and their effects on family behavior and relationships. . . ." (p. 27).

Unlike other studies of work-family interaction which more commonly employ class or nature of occupation as key variables, this study emphasizes space as a distinguishing criterion. More narrowly, it focuses on shared home-workspace. It is this sharing of space rather than the nature of the particular occupation which is paramount. Thus, throughout the book I use the terms "home work," "work-at-home families," and "home-working families" interchangeably to designate families using shared space. Readers should be cautioned, however, that these are not perceived as neutral terms by many scholars. Reading those words, a labor historian might focus on the exploited immigrant home worker of the early twentieth century, laboring in sweatshop conditions. Marxist scholars might focus on the patriarchal relations reproduced in this gender-inequitable system. Family economists might dwell upon the cash-producing but often unacknowledged labor of the farm wife or the array of small income-generating sidelines often attached to farm life. Entrepreneurs might point out the phenomenal growth in self-employed women over the past decade, many of whom base their businesses in the home. Futurists might allude to the actual and predicted growth in telecommuting, computer-based work which allows people to work in flexiplace settings rather than a centralized workplace. Observers of rural life might single out the small cottage industries present in kitchens, barns, and shops. Given the diversity of circumstances under which home work occurs, many interpretations are possible; correspondingly, scholars have developed a variety of terms reflecting aspects of home work most familiar to them. These specialized terms range from industrial home work and outwork, which usually convey a negative flavor, to home-based employment, cottage industry, at home income generation, and telecommuting which each convey distinctive nuances.

I have tried to address some of these complex definitions of home work in chapter 2. However, consistent with the microfamily focus in this book, I have used home-working families simply as a term to describe shared family and work space. Chapter 4 more fully relates how these home-working families encounter space.

The interactive model for studying work and family recognizes diversity, exploring how families in different circumstances encounter work. Importantly, it supports the idea that families are not simply passive outcomes of work influences but can in turn alter and shape work experiences themselves. Its deliberate focus on the mechanisms of integration between the two is new. Home work exemplifies one strategy for integrating and as such merits closer study as it reveals how some contemporary families encounter and respond to work.

Chapter 1

Pursuing Integration

You have these goals for yourself and your family—
Whether it's financial or emotional or whatever,
you have these goals. Some people work at tam-
ing these goals and some people don't. And I
think the people who are out in the work-a-day
world can't possibly work at effectively reaching
the other goals, you know, the other parts of
their life, but I think this is as close as I can get.
(A home-working father)

Viewed through the narrowest of lenses, home-working
families differ from other working families on only one dimension: that of workspace location. Unlike most Americans
who work in separate offices, factories, shops, or schools,
home-based workers derive their incomes working in their
home's living room, kitchen, shop, or office. Beyond this simple
distinction of workspace location, home work occupations
resemble conventional positions in name and content. Historically, home workers have been seamstresses, insurance agents,
farmers, craftspeople, doctors, mechanics, babysitters, "mom-
and-pop" store owners, writers. In this study they include
machine knitters, a mechanic, chef, day care provider, veterinarian, art dealer, hairdresser, flytyer, seamstress, translator,
secretary, cabinetmaker. Thus, home workers' occupations per
se are neither remarkable nor wildly divergent from the work
experiences shared by many other Americans and the content
of their work would be familiar to workers laboring in traditional, separate workplaces.

Numerically, home-working families described in this
book represent only a small proportion of the working popu-

lation in America: estimates suggest that 5%–10% of workers
are home-based. Other figures cite a possible 10 million regular home workers, and an additional 10–12 million who perform at least part of their work at home (Herbers 1986). A
1985 Bureau of Labor Statistics study more precisely identified 8.4 million people who work at home in excess of eight
hours weekly in non-farm jobs (Horvath 1986). The fact that
such estimates are best construed from a minor, long-form
census question regarding commuting distances to work
attests to our nearly universal assumption that home and
workplace are physically separate. Studies of work life in
contemporary society routinely proceed on the supposition
that home and worklife are physically distinct and consequently emotionally remote as well. Although working at
home was once a norm in early America, twentieth-century
life has rendered it an anomaly. Now an aberration, an exception to the expected work pattern, home workers have more
recently included the atypical: at one extreme, the immigrant—exploited, slaving at putting-out work in home sweatshops, a practice substantially reduced by social reformers of
the 1930s. At the other anomalous extreme, it has included
farmers living out the nostalgic ideal of family togetherness, a
cherished image no longer considered functional for late
twentieth-century family lives. In between, a sprinkling of
other more recent work-at-home anomalies have included
women with small children, persons with handicapping conditions, small or family-businesspeople and craftspeople. Few
of these, excepting possibly farmers, have garnered much attention from researchers. The curious blend of numerical in-
significance and anomalous status combine to make them
non-representative and therefore uninteresting to traditional
social science research which typically strives for maximum
generalizability across large numbers. Occupationally, home
workers are unexceptional; the kinds of work they perform
are also readily observed in the work world's conventional settings which are far more accessible and amenable to group
examination. Overwhelmingly, researchers have concentrated
their efforts on workers in this very conventional, organized,
public setting.

Reverting to the narrow lens focus, then, the simple distinction of workspace location offers unremarkable specimens
for study. However, the richness in this culture is not to be

found simply in an obvious reading of workspace location. Instead, one must peer beyond to observe the fertile natural laboratory these families offer for the study of work and family in contemporary America and, most particularly, how they act out one of the most powerfully appealing themes in contemporary writing: the integration of work and family. To spurn the study of such families as numerically insignificant or statistically non-representative ignores a rich source of experience exemplifying how some families attempt to balance, juggle, and otherwise attain the euphemisms representing harmony between two frequently conflicting domains. The struggle to reconcile the two arenas occupies centerstage both in popular magazines which chronicle the dilemmas of the working mother, and in academic journals which address the very same issues though in a more aloof tone. Plainly, the outpouring of writing, conferencing, agitating, reforming, demanding, and individual agonizing manifests the difficulty faced by working parents in alleviating tensions between work and family lives. At this point in time, solutions are less in evidence than are the indicators of stress.

Home-working families, in blending work and family lives, offer one of the few existing concrete opportunities to examine this powerful theme of integration. Their choice of a distinctive work style makes them not non-representative, but instead highly illustrative of one strategy of integrating. The details of their daily lives embody and lend substance to the hazily defined but intuitively appealing concept of integration. Importantly, their lives offer some precision, an initial contribution to defining pragmatically what integration might signify for American families. Additionally, beyond the very pragmatic outlines of integration they offer, their lives link integration to broad issues implicit in discussing the concept: integration as historically (and currently) women's work, workplace reform's effect on family lives, changes in the nature of work, the role of children in the work-family balance, and the reconnection of the relationship between work and family. Thus, the importance of home-working families lies not in their numerical representativeness but in the applied lesson in integrating work and family lives which they can offer. Of greatest value is not how closely they imitate the lives of conventional American workers but rather in how they diverge from the common pattern

INTEGRATION: LINKING WORK AND LOVE

> I feel good about my family. If I went out to work,
> I wouldn't, and if I didn't do anything at all, I
> wouldn't. (A home knitter)

> Well, they're (home-working parents) not in such
> a rush when you get home from school . . . they
> (other working parents) don't have time for you.
> (Nine-year-old child of home-working mother)

These comments from a home-working parent and a child express some of the conflicts undermining a harmonious balance between work and family life. The difficulty inherent in creating and sustaining a sense of adequacy as individual, worker, spouse, and parent is a common theme in late twentieth-century academic and popular writing. Whether describing pressures on working mothers, advocating pragmatic innovations in work patterns, agitating for increased government support for working families, or detailing individual efforts to balance, these writings share an implicit ideal of greater integration between work and family life. The existence of such a desirable goal is also tacitly expressed in the considerable body of social science research examining imbalances, or obstacles to work-family integration. Detailing impediments to integration such as inadequate child care facilities, inflexible work patterns, or insufficient time to fulfill both work and family responsibilities, implies that reversing such imbalances will provide a more equable relationship, a more satisfying ideal.

Curiously, integration as a concept has been enthusiastically embraced but minimally examined. Its novelty as an implicit goal is quite recent, emerging from the powerful social revolution effected by women's entry into the paid labor force. Prior to the 1970s, integration played virtually no role in a work drama where men held the leading parts. Quite to the contrary, segregation between work and family lives was the expectation as the links between working and loving were ignored. Work was examined principally through intraoccupational characteristics, and the idea that work and family could mutually influence one another was a foreign one (Kanter 1977). Despite a few pioneering efforts to suggest that there was indeed interplay between work and family, the prevailing assumption in social science literature was that work was compartmentalized, physically and emotionally distinct from family life. Thus, work and family lives were ascribed naturally different characteristics: "the prevailing tendency is to consider work synonymous with occupational involvement and intimacy synonymous with family and personal attachment" (Richardson 1981, 38). Correspondingly, the work world was a virtually exclusive male realm in which occupational achievement drew the most attention as researchers studied intra-occupational characteristics of work (content, satisfaction, rewards, performance), economic and social structural aspects, public policy, and, more philosophically, the very nature of work. The very few studies that even admitted a connecting link to family were those focusing on the effects of the workplace on the family, such as demands made upon the family by the husband's job (for example, Hannah Papenek's (1973) conception of the "two person career"), effects on child rearing arising from conditions of the father's job (Kohn, *Class and Conformity* 1977), or family dynamics engendered by economically determined class position. Fittingly, family research complemented this men's instrumental work world approach as it investigated the family's expressive function, rarely crossing boundaries. Men, in charge of the work world, were freed to act instrumentally by women's assumption of expressive roles at home. The rightness of such a gender-based model of work went basically unquestioned, sustained by a theory of structural-functionalism which subscribed to the necessity and naturalness of such a division of labor.

This rigid compartmentalization of work and family lives weakened and then collapsed with the dramatic influx of women into men's previously inviolate work domain. Not only were walls breached, but a torrent of new voices flooded that workplace, demanding for the first time that family needs receive some consideration from employers. Connections were no longer to be ignored or denied but instead articulated and responded to with some sensitivity. Researchers, scrambling to react to this extraordinary social change, began examining the history of work and family research, noting its deficiencies, and advocating that attention be given to the links between working and loving (Kanter 1977). In tandem, working women and researchers looked at these connections while several factors contributed to the demise of segregated lives as an implicit standard. First, the unprecedented entry of married women into the workplace—and particularly married women with children—forced attention to their voices. Early on, researchers acknowledged the relationship between work and family needs among women, recognizing the "shifting but always symbiotic nature of women's household and workplace labor" (diLeonardo 1985, 491). Over the past decade, research into women's work has clarified this "shifting but always symbiotic" relationship by examining links with family lives and job satisfaction, maternal role and employment variables, sources of stress in conflicting work and parent roles, and specific needs of working single parent and dual-career families. Although investigation of this special relationship remains a prime area of research interest, there is little consensus as to its origin. Women's work and family lives apparently affect each other reciprocally and compellingly but contention exists as to whether such linkage emanates from biological, psychological, sociological, economic, or philosophical sources.

Another blow to the segregated ideal came from feminist research into women's historical work patterns. The striking finding was not that "women have always worked" (Kessler-Harris 1981) but rather the startling multiplicity of ways in which they had always worked. Unlike men, whose industrial work patterns were fairly uniform and who set the implicit standard definition of work, women's work has been characterized by remarkable diversity. Part-time work, seasonal labor, varying life cycle employment, unpaid family labor, putting-out work, taking in boarders, farm work, and factory labor on "mother's hours" all provide examples of distinctive work patterns. The unifying key to this array of work styles lay in married women's efforts to blend work and family needs, to integrate rather than segregate demands from each realm. In contrast, we have as yet little evidence that men might have followed a similar pattern.

Research on contemporary women's work continues to recognize the intertwining of women's work and family lives, whether the topic is dual-career couples, or concrete ways in which women "bring their families to the shop floor" (Lamphere 1985). Glaringly, with a few notable exceptions, little comparable research exists on the intertwining of men's work and family lives. Integration is primarily a women's issue, prompted by women's entry into the labor force and explored by researchers delving into women's life experiences. Much of what we deduce about integration emanates from popular and academic discussions of impediments to integration, from the difficulties intrinsic to balancing, juggling, or evening out the demands of working and loving. Thus, although an ideal of work-family integration has emerged from the shadows, details of how it might work for families remain obscure. On the one hand, for many working families integration remains a glowing though intuitive ideal; on the other, some theoreticians argue that it represents a dark link to women's past, an obstacle to progress. The patterns of connectedness between working and loving are finally receiving attention, a remarkable debut in a relatively few years. However, there is little clarity on the nature or future of such links as controversy continues over whether such a linkage represents a backward or forward step for women. Whether men share any similar interests in integrating is a subject only tentatively being addressed. Further, integration is itself only imprecisely defined (primarily through negatives) and we have little sense of what a more integrated life would actually encompass for working families. As yet, no clear alternative has replaced the fallen standard of the segregated life. Instead, we have a series of links which provide clues to what such a life might entail, and the experiences of atypical families such as home workers to offer some substance to a rather vague though intuitively appealing notion. Several of these links, which may enhance our understanding, are explored in the following pages.

LINK: IMAGES OF INTEGRATION

Cultural images may either reflect reality or exalt an unattainable ideal. Briefly reviewing some of its public images allows us to gather a sense of integration's appeal and also where the pitfalls may lie in constructing it as a model. The historically preceding image—that of the work-centered male and the home-dwelling female—represents a social myth of great durability and longevity. Rooted in the nineteenth century when, for the first time, woman's role as mother was separated out from her other roles, glorified and isolated, the notion of separate and gender-appropriate spheres developed. It was man's duty to tangle with the harsh realities of an industrializing world while women were entrusted with the special role of creating a haven from that cruel, mercenary domain. Previous historical roles where women had fulfilled vital economic functions and men had shared in family responsibilities were ignored in favor of the new arrangement. Although this was by no means the experience of all women of all races and classes, the imagery prevailed and endured, affecting women and families for more than one hundred years. Naturally, the domestic woman was a fitting complement to the working man and the rightness of such a model went essentially unquestioned until the rise of the feminist movement in the 1960s. Women who did not or could not fit into this highly compartmentalized, segregated model were viewed as aberrant. Researchers from the 1930s onward sustained this image of the segregated ideal by ironically juxtaposing their investigations of family and work, concentrating on the problems engendered by the unemployed male and the employed female. ("From the mid-1930s, when studies of the topic first appeared, almost all of the published studies focused on the presumed deleterious influence on the child of the mother's working outside of the home" Bronfenbrenner and Crouter 1982, 43).

The crumbling of the work-family segregation ideal opened the gates for an influx of competing models. Although ensuing ideals varied in content, they acknowledged a common concern with the interrelationship between work and family life, thus challenging the model which had maintained their separateness. For the first time, the public model conceded that work and family do not exist in isolation but rather interact in complex balance with the parent-worker as the fulcrum. Not coincidentally, interest in integration developed as women entered the labor force, colliding with a work world long attuned to men's values. For the first time, too, research interest swung from the prescribed and isolated world of men's work to the far more complex world of women's work which invariably seemed to spill over into spousal and parental arenas. No longer were researchers concentrating on the narrow focus of the intraoccupational world; instead, they reoriented to issues of women's wider world as they developed new techniques to deal with a more intricate relationship.

One of the first new integrated images to emerge from this change in work-family relationships was the much-touted Supermom of the 1970s. The Supermom was indeed a model of integration as it clearly acknowledged woman's dual responsibilities in the work and family realms. (There was no Superdad counterpart). This model glorified the woman who not only integrated but did it all perfectly. The ease with which the Supermom graciously and efficiently balanced conflicting demands clashed with the real life experience of most working women but nonetheless attested to integration's inherent appeal. For such mythical individuals as Supermoms, linking working and loving was simply a matter of over-achievement in both arenas, rather tyrannically leading working women to believe that they could indeed have it all. Such a model, of course, masks pragmatic obstacles to having it all, such as child care availability and reliability, presence or absence or spousal support, and limitations on human time, energy, and financial resources. Ironically and insidiously, it suggested that women could integrate by being schizophrenic; that women could succeed on the job by being male-like and conversely in the home by being female-like, experiencing no conflict between two competitive realms. Integration was to be achieved by aligning two disparate worlds, recognizing their demands, and then giving each its due while not crossing boundaries.

Gradually, the Supermom ideal eroded in the face of reality, giving way to other models of integration. Subsequent models were a bit more wary, acknowledging rather than obscuring the conflicts inherent in fulfilling work and family commitments. More recently, the emergent model has been The Juggler as popular magazines promote an array of titles dealing with pragmatic issues for working women: assessing child care options, handling burn-out, choosing flexible work patterns, assigning household chores and dealing with guilt.

Articles of this genre frequently employ "balance" or "juggle" in their titles, handy euphemisms for integrating. Characteristic of the acknowledged difficulties in integrating has been a concern with options: as pragmatic issues are discussed so are the variety of possible responses. Single-parent, female headed households have different needs and resources than dual-career families; variations in marital status, class, race, ages and number of children all contribute to a far more pluralistic discussion of balancing. The range of integrating options even includes choosing not to work, a recent subject of heated discussion among women in books and articles. Juggling is subsumed under the category of integration, assuming its desirability, but adding diversity and intricacy to the model.

More recently, images of integration have emerged from other sources, providing new facets to the image while still maintaining it as an ideal. Significantly, for the first time, men are being drawn into the model as popular articles begin to portray their efforts at integrating work and family responsibilities. As writers single out men who adjust their work lives to accommodate family needs (Gregg, 1986), balancing, previously an exclusively female task, shows some signs of crossing gender lines. Portrayals of such integrated men, however, still focus on their uniqueness while the corresponding assumption for women is that integration is an implicit albeit frustratingly elusive expectation. Accordingly, social science research is still examining the juggling woman (the vast preponderance of work-family literature deals with women's roles) while only beginning to investigate the interplay of these realms for men.

A larger backdrop to men's forays into the family-work nexus is provided by one final image: that of the symmetrical family. First described by Willmot and Young (1973), symmetrical families are those in which parents most fully integrate their work and family roles, where tasks and responsibilities are most completely shared and gender roles are little differentiated. Perhaps the truest form of integration, representing a continuation of the ideal to its fullest, there is little indication as yet of its widespread adoption. Most research indicates no sweeping rush by men to enter the juggling sweepstakes, although modest advances are noted in task-sharing by some observers. Essentially, women's expansion into the work role has not been equally paralleled by men's fuller adoption of household responsibilities. Integration is still largely a female endeavor.

Arguably, then, the ideal of integration of work and family life has captured the imagination if not the full participation of many working families. Attaining a harmonious balance which allows the parent-worker to satisfy commitments in both areas is widely perceived as a desirable goal. As yet, few concrete indicators exist to point the way to accomplishing such a goal. Understanding integration's origin, function, and relation to home work requires searching for its sources in several distinct fields. Then, by drawing together these varied sources, a clearer outline emerges.

LINK: PRAGMATIC WORK INNOVATIONS

> Several aspects of work must be restructured. First, the deep split between home and work must be healed. The split is not only spatial but is also one of values . . . and structure. Second, the rigidity of work-time requirements . . . must be eased. . . . Third, work needs to be organized less hierarchically. (Boneparth and Stoper 1983, 266)

> I would never go back to work in the shoeshop again as long as I live—unless it was between that and not eating. It would have to get to that point before I'd ever go into any kind of factory work. When my girls are a little older, however, I'm going to try to get them to go in, and cure them good too. (A home-working mother)

> I can't stand to have somebody stand over my back and give me orders all the time. You know, a boss expects you to do it his way. You have your own way of doing it that will come out exactly the same, but, no, you've got to do it his way. And I can't hack it. (A home-working father)

> And then there are no time deadlines either— there is no late for work or trying to get away

early in the traffic. And I don't have to get all
dressed up every day, which is something I
don't like to do. (A home-working mother)

Tentative workplace innovations aimed at accommodating
rather than ignoring family needs marked a turnabout in employer philosophy during the 1970s. Prior to that decade, per-
sonnel services primarily confined themselves to intraoccupational categories: hiring and firing, promotions and
advances, inservice training, and other activities revolving
around the worker himself or herself. Occasionally, enlight-
ened employers offered additional services aimed at ameliorat-
ing the employee's problems affecting work performance (such
as alcoholism counseling) but such efforts typically centered
on the individual alone. Consistent with the segregated work
ideal, little connecting with family life occurred as employees
were expected to devote their time exclusively to job-related
needs.

Such a quiet denial of family connections to the work
world was rudely disrupted by women's entry into the work
force. Women, bringing their family concerns with them, agitated for accommodating rather than disregarding family
needs. Over scarcely more than a decade, family issues invaded a workplace consciousness long free from such considerations. The need for reliable, quality day care was one of the
earliest issues negotiated as some employers began providing
on-site, voucher system, or referral day care services. Their reluctant willingness to do so tacitly recognized that the days of
segregation were over. Day care was just the beginning, however, as a female workers raised other family related issues:
parental leave policies, sick child leave, part time and other
flexible hour patterns, job sharing and counseling services
for family needs. Some employers, responding to employee demands, instituted human resource services which acknowledged and treated family-related problems. Even feminists,
who previously had distanced themselves from women's family issues, joined the coalition seeking broader economic and
social support for working families, signaling their recognition as well as the integrated model.

Tentative forays into workplace reform as a cure for the
conflict of women's work and family needs have led to innova-

tive patterns which increase time flexibility: flextime, job sharing, four-day weeks, and other variable work scheduling endeavors. However, despite research showing support for major restructuring of current work patterns (Best 1978), most proposals designed to ameliorate work-family conflict merely tinker with minor adjustments in the family's ability to accommodate work demands. More radical proposals which might fundamentally alter the nature of work—such as encouraging home-based rather than centralized work settings—have not been widely adopted. Despite futurists' rosy predictions, the electronic cottage has not become widespread. Many of the objections to such home work spring from managers who worry that flexiplace will shortcircuit their ability to supervise, command, and/or keep appropriate tabs on their employees. Such concerns indicate a line being drawn between workplace reforms which accommodate some family needs and those which too radically and unacceptably restructure the work world. Whether the impetus for integration can override such a fundamental philosophical difference remains to be seen. One measure of its success as an ideal will be seen in the proliferation of work-flexibility schemes which emerge over the next few years. As a tangible expression of an ideal, workplace reforms offer one of the few concrete pointers to its boundaries.

Employers responding to requests for more flexible work time patterns are indeed answering one of working parents' most oft-cited needs since time conflicts appear repeatedly as stressors in research. However, some other more subtle changes are also occurring as a result of women's entry into the workplace. Some writers suggest that women hold alternative work values, subscribing to a philosophy of cooperation, concern for others, the value of intrinsic reward, and a sense of interdependent concern for others. Such values, if present, clash strikingly with traditional emphases on competition, individuality, status hierarchy, and extrinsic reward which long fueled the work world. The infusion of such alternative values potentially could create a new work world culture, representing a different form of integration. In such a context, one could argue that the few simple workplace reforms which have already occurred represent one toehold of this alternative value set, with more radical restructuring to come. Whether all women do indeed share such interests, and whether they ascend to wield enough power to institute such reforms is only conjectural at present. There is research evidence that men who subscribe to nontraditional sex role beliefs also share interest in more radical work world restructuring and a coalition could produce some surprising results.

Arguing that a revolution in workplace values is indeed imminent are futurists such as Alan Toffler whose *The Third Wave* (1980) predicted a radical decentralizing and restructuring of the workplace as the United States economy shifts fundamentally from manufacturing to information-processing. One of the first popularizers of the electronic cottage, Toffler pictured a resurgence of work-at-home opportunities as an expression of this elemental reorientation in values. The rebirth and dramatic growth of home work is "so potentially revolutionary and so alien to our experience, it needs far more attention than it has received so far" (Toffler 1980, 216–217). Enthusiastically, he predicts that "the electronic cottage may turn out to be the characteristic mom-and-pop business of the future . . ." leading "to a new work-together family unit involving children . . ." (p. 372). Among the positive, enriching consequences he predicts for family life: a closer, more intimate marital relationship, more equitable sharing of household chores, meaningful opportunities for children to participate in work, and a generally expanded, more intense level of family interaction.

Nor is Toffler alone in his enthusiasm. A feminist perspective is offered by Boneparth and Stoper (1983) who suggest that the reintroduction of paid work into the home could break down the gender division of labor by blurring the rigidities between men's and women's work and promoting more flexible sharing of labor across work and household responsibilities. Women's magazines frequently feature portraits of successful, home-based businesswomen and "how-to" articles designed to assist women in setting up at home. Journalistic articles promoting the electronic cottage abound, with stories describing how "Home Computers Are Nuturing Working Mothers" (Faries 1983), accompanied by glowing predictions of a vast labor force of at-home workers, primarily mothers of young children. Beyond descriptions of the relatively limited number of such programs, there has been little research on what actually happens when work moves into the home. Is the product truly the rosy, enriched family life predicted by Toffler, or merely a continued ghettoization of women's work? Demanding exploration are questions such as how will workers allocate time and space to work and family? Which gets precedence in a crisis? How are other family members involved? How does child care figure into the work-family equation? Until the actual mechanics of home work are examined, speculation holds sway.

LINK: CHILDREN

> It's my philosophy. Men have been taken out of parenting—I don't know if it happened with the Industrial Revolution or it's just that women are smarter. But anyway, that's a place that Charles is involved—with them. I think it teaches them responsibility, some place where he has to put up with the mess too and deal with it, and they have to learn that he is human. (Wife of a home worker)

> So Lori (at six months of age) would go along and ride in the truck. If I was going in the barn I would take her in with me and I set her in the hay so she'd be out of the way, particularly if we were going to have to catch a calf or something like that. (A home-working father)

Children, of course, are at the heart of the collision between work and family worlds. It is their arrival and presence which precipitates conflicts and impels choices in the most palpable of ways. Children's needs have generated most workplace reforms (parental leave, day care, sick child care, flextime), created the most stress in working parents attempting to reconcile their needs, and served to actualize work-family conflict in hundreds of immediate, routine ways. Children are at the heart of the integration model because it is principally parental demands which require the juggling of work and family roles. Women, particularly, have long innovated responses to the work environment in order to accommodate children's needs, choosing to adapt work schedules, change jobs or diverge from standard work-week expectations in order to respond to those needs. The remarkable diversity historically evidenced in women's work arrangements is largely compelled by the presence of young children.

Curiously however, we know very little about children's contribution to work-family interaction. Despite their critical link in the integration chain, children's perceptions of work are rarely addressed, their opinions or conceptions of their parents' work sought out (Bloom-Feshbach, Bloom-Feshbach and Heller 1982). Although major protagonists in the drama, children play virtually silent roles throughout. Integration of work and family roles presumably requires input from children but as yet that input has not been scripted. As a result, we know almost nothing of children's opinions or perceptions of work and family interaction.

Several factors account for our failure to solicit children's input directly. Some researchers cite methodological reasons, specifically theoretical frameworks about work which are oriented solely to adults. Others cite the lack of good interview methodology to use with young children, the absence of cooperation by children, and a wish to avoid discomfort to parents about having their children interviewed (Lein 1974; Piotrkowski 1978). More probably, children have been unaddressed because they are not perceived as fulfilling any logical economic function, having been assigned expressive roles instead. Thus, rather than seeing work and family as mutually infusing (and conceding children's roles in that mutuality), most researchers continue to perpetuate the image of man's work effects on the family, a view from which children are excluded. Consequently, children are most commonly utilized by researchers as dependent variables, as outcomes of some facet of their parent's job.

Studies which do address children operate from this latter paradigm. Even such a widely acknowledged and applauded work as Kohn's *Class and Conformity* (1977) which examined the specific effects on childrearing of the context of the father's workplace fits this model. Such research made no effort to look either at the intervening steps from job to childrearing values (a path which seems to lead through the mother as well) or to ask children how they perceive their father's work.

Even findings which implicate children most directly, such as studies of maternal guilt and stress around dual roles, generally fail to solicit children's direct input. Repeatedly, adult responses proxy for children's, leaving our direct knowledge of children's perceptions of their parents' work meager and adult-interpreted. The limited research that does straightforwardly solicit children's own observations deals almost exclusively with children over the age of seven; children of preschool age are virtually ignored despite the fact that it is their tender age that most directly and acutely affects parent-work role equilibrium.

For most American children, then, their parents' work is a foreign culture, physically inaccessible, cognitively unfamiliar and emotionally distant. Bronfenbrenner (1979) places parental work in the exosystem for most children—that distant arena which certainly affects children's development but with which they have no direct interaction. Kanter (1977, 77) parallels this reasoning by stating, "It has often been suggested that the development of children is impaired by their inability to see their parents' work." Exactly what it is that children are expected to perceive or construct as a result of involvement with the work world is not entirely clear. Until research on work and family matters directly involves children of all ages, the question of how and why it might be beneficial to them is unanswered.

Ironically, then, children exist at the nexus of the work-family connection but as passive participants in the eyes of most social science research, their contribution to that complicated tangle virtually ignored. A suggestion as to why social science has discounted the child's involvement in the work world as anything other than a dependent variable emanates from historians looking at how the nature of work has changed. Commonly, contemporary work studies focus on the simple fact of employment vs. non-employment as an independent variable (for example, effects of maternal employment on children) rather than examining the nature or context of that work, or its meaning to the participants. Historians, taking a longer range view, examine this gap by focusing on the changing nature of work. In contrast to more recent theorists who see work as a static, uniform category from which deductions are made about effects on children, Stern, Smith and Doolittle (1975) maintain that when work and family were most thoroughly integrated in pre-industrial America, childrearing and work were continuous, that "childrearing enhanced rather than detracted from adult work and leisure" (p. 97). When children assisted in home production, and when educating them was harmonious and continuous with working at home, then no conflict existed. The twentieth century, removing work from the home, produced a conflict for parents, forcing them to make a choice between "spending time with their children and spending time at work or play" (Stern et al. 1975, 98), resulting in an "opportunity cost" of having children. This change in the nature of work, while perhaps providing insight into why social science has tended to ignore children's input into work and viewed work-family in opposition, raises other issues to consider. If children are economically and socially divorced from the work world, then where and when do they suddenly become socialized for it? If such an opportunity cost exists, how do working parents reconcile/mediate such a deficit?

LINK: WOMEN'S WORK, MEN'S WORK, FAMILY WORK

> The separate workplace also represented for men a possible retreat from intimacy, as it may continue to do today for some people. (Kanter 1977, 14)

> Finally, in female work choices both old and new, an extraordinary personal element seems to predominate, a desire for a warm human relationship at work. This obviously fits the preference for a home or shop industry where familial or friendly contacts can be assumed. . . . Women wanted to work in or near a family context, within the home where possible. (Branca 1975, 141, 146)

> Women have always had that tradition—they've been brought up having a thousand and one little jobs to do around the house every day. And sometimes you can't fulfill them all, or you can't even fulfill one individual one, but you have to

attack each problem as it comes up. . . . The
time is very fluid for a woman. It's like the tide
going in and out, whereas for a man it's like a
drawbridge coming down and going up. (Househusband of a home worker)

For most of this century, studying work meant studying
men. Feminist scholarship and popular writing of the past fifteen years altered this direction, discovering and sharpening
distinctions between men's and women's work experiences.
The new social history explored the richness and diversity of
women's work, an array so varied it could not be forced into
the mold cast by men. Unpaid work (for example, household
labor or volunteer work), part-time employment, seasonal labor, varying life cycle employment related to the presence of
children, labor unrecognized or unrecorded by census (such
as a farm wife), taking in boarders, working mother's hours,
completing putting-out or home work, all reflect important
ways in which women contributed to the economic functioning of their households. Few of these work styles conform to
our standard expectations about work created by the male experience—that it be remunerated, consistent, uninterrupted,
conferring of identity and status, and unaffected by personal
or familial needs. What such pluralistic work patterns do represent is "women's distinctive ability to initiate changes in
work roles, even in traditional settings" (Branca 1975, 129).

The impetus to innovate arose from women's efforts to
reconcile family and work needs. Men, essentially freed from
household labor and child care in the nineteenth century, sev-
ered the links between work and family; women, historically
responsible for family life and economic support, acknowledged the connections between working and loving and developed strategies to do justice to both.

Current researchers, agreeing that married women's work
efforts have been shaped by family demands, have burrowed
into the complexity of this relationship, searching for insight.
Although accord exists on the historical intertwining of work
and family needs, there is no unanimity as to its cause or effect. Some historians argue persuasively that women's efforts
to integrate are a sign of strength and healthy balance while
describing richly the combinations of family strategy em-

ployed by women to manuever among competing demands. Countering voices decry the dual burden foisted on women by a sexist society, urging a restructuring of the family to free women from such responsibility. What is clear is that, in contrast with earlier research on men's work which isolated the workplace from the familial setting, research on women's work invariably connects the two. Topics addressed range from theoretical discussions as to why work and family have always been "two worlds in one" for women (E. Pleck 1976), to heavily pragmatic studies of the difficulty of reconciling prevalent in contemporary social science. Consonant with this research emphasis linking women, work, and family roles is the voluminous literature on maternal employment effects on children which has no comparable echo in men's work research. Indeed, the comparison of the two produces diametrical assumptions—that women should be present in the home with their children (and consequently prodigious research is required to prove that they should be free to work) and, conversely, that men should be absent from the home. The latter assumption has seen little research, aside from general father-absent research more commonly dealing with total absence due to death, divorce, or desertion. Questions about the inevitability and desirability of father absence from the home due to work remain unexamined.

At the core of the women's work/men's work discussion lies the relative valuing of work and family life. Some historians maintain that women have always organized their work life around their family needs, accommodating work to family rather than the reverse pattern more typical of men's work; certainly contemporary social science research pursues this theme subtly but tenaciously in its continued focus on women's multiple role balancing in contrast to men's. Attempts to determine empirically whether women position family responsibilities higher than work, or whether women value family more than men, are few in nature and, according to one analysis, pervaded by sexist bias. Feldberg and Glenn's analysis of literature dealing with men, women, and their work claims that male research is based on a job model which relates to the "work people do as the primary independent variable" while women's work is a gender-based model where "women's relationship to employment is treated as derivative of personal characteristics and relationships to family situations" (Feld-berg and Glenn 1982, 66–67). This subtle bias which infuses research on men's and women's work does not provide an equal basis for comparing how men and women value their work life relative to their family life. Thus, women's work and family roles will be inevitably and unfairly joined, an inequi-table linkage from which men escape. In this view, an inte-grated model only spells continued exploitation for women unless men move symmetrically to assume more household and child care labor.

A scattering of studies is now beginning to examine this interplay for men, but such efforts are heavily outweighed by the ponderous and pessimistic studies outlining the difficulty of integrating for women. Joseph Pleck, who has been follow-ing this issue for several years, maintains that there are signs of change, although no observer is mentioning any whole-hearted rush by men to assume household and child care la-bor. Utilizing answers to questions about work and family life from the 1977 Quality of Employment Survey, Pleck suggests that "men's family role is far more psychologically significant to them than is their work role" contrary to stereotypes about "men obsessed by work and oblivious to the family" (Pleck and Lang 1978, 29). Related studies, while not explicitly ad-dressing the family/work role valuation, have pointed out that men have increased their family roles somewhat, particularly in creating innovative solutions to parenting demands neces-sitated by the wife's employment. Often this change in bal-ance is not deliberately sought but may be thrust upon men as a resolution to a family conflict; Hood and Golden (1979) described how differential shift scheduling allowed husband and wife to avoid day care by sharing parenting responsibili-ties, resulting in positive consequences for the father and his children. Lein's (1974) work also emphasized how frequently parents attempted to work different shifts in order to avoid using day care, thereby increasing her working fathers' family roles. Aside from these almost serendipitous findings, little direct work has been done to examine men's family/work bal-ances, particularly on the microsocial level, the consensus of most writing still being that women bear the burden of the dual role demands while men chiefly enact the one work role. Such an exclusive focus on women as balancers creates little helpful information about men's family-work integration efforts.

Perhaps more importantly, since so little research occurs on the microsocial level, we know very little about how individual families are negotiating the interplay of women's work, men's work, and family work. Most social research emanates from large-scale survey, leaving hidden the specific techniques by which families adapt to or resist changes in work and family patterns. Although recent research has illumined the very distinctive approaches characterizing women's work, men's work-family interplay has remained obscured. Children's input into the work-family equation is, as noted, virtually absent. Until these research inequities are righted, clarifying the women's work, men's work, and family work relationship will be exceptionally difficult.

LINK: GENDER ROLES

> Besides allowing men and women to better integrate their work and family roles, work at home . . . could help break down the sexual division of labor. If men's work were located in women's traditional sphere, the home, the psychological distinction between women's work and men's work could be lessened. (Boneparth and Stoper 1983, 271)

> Even my boys, if I was sitting there knitting when they were tiny, they learned the work—and they all knit. In fact, the one who lives up in Caribou has made three quilts. . . . He knits— they've got one baby and he knit his mittens and hat. . . . A family that doesn't cooperate—if a man thinks that she has her place and he has his place, she does her work and he does his work—that wouldn't fit there at all. (A home knitter)

Argument over men's and women's work represents only a limited portion of a much wider debate about gender roles in contemporary society. Women's encroachment upon men's traditional and exclusive workplace sphere represents this role clash perhaps most acutely, attacking men's power directly by competing for jobs, and insidiously by exposing work values alternative to men's. Resistance and confusion in the workplace exemplify the underlying struggle to re-define gender role, and efforts to integrate represent the larger struggle. The pervasive influence of gender role expectations on women's work and family lives is accentuated by studies repeatedly demonstrating the importance to women of adequately fulfilling responsibilities as a parent, worker, and spouse. Whether studying child care issues, time scheduling conflicts, marital stress, or workplace responsivity, women's wish to attain a reasonably harmonious balance comes through consistently. Critically, however, women still place much of the responsibility or blame for imbalance upon themselves, indicating that they still subscribe to both the old and new gender role expectations. Studies indicate that women still retain responsibility for household labor, child care, and paid employment with spouses functioning more as assistants rather than equal task sharers. There is some suggestion that traditional divisions of labor in the household continue to exist partly because men are not clamoring to take them on, and partly because women may be reluctant to cede their customary roles. One study of coping strategies among professional women with children found that such women essentially seek resolution to conflict within themselves rather than through outside support. Here, women experiencing conflict among multiple demands most frequently chose resolution through "increased role behavior," that is working harder and more efficiently (for example, Supermom) rather than allocating responsibility or seeking resolution through negotiation with others (Elman and Gilbert 1984). Such a conflict resolution may exemplify women's ongoing dilemma or merely reflect social reality. Unquestionably the gender role crunch still most acutely pressures women on a personal level.

Other writers seeking answers to gender role distinctions look beyond the personal balancing tangle in which women enmesh themselves. Some allocate responsibility to the economic system, particularly capitalism. Matthei (1982) maintains that capitalism fostered and reflected a rigid sexual division of labor, emerging from a colonial family economy when sex roles per se had not been so markedly differentiated.

By placing women in the private sphere of the home and exalting their homemaking skills, women became consumers, useful purchasers of the products created by men in the industrialized world. However, this convenient arrangement contained the seeds of its own destruction, for women had to increase consumption standards to purchase all that industry could create. As consumption standards increased, however, husbands' wages could no longer cover the cost of purchasing such a variety of necessities and women began to enter the work force in order to acquire these perceived necessities for their own families. Initially, then, married women were entering the workplace protected by the legitimate guise of fulfilling her seemly role as homemaker, undertaking wage work in order to respond to family needs. Such a seemingly inoffensive entry transformed itself into today's dual career or two-paycheck families where women's incomes may superficially be designated the secondary or extra wage but are nonetheless a potent tool of women's assertion within the family. Matthei goes on to suggest that the breakdown of the sexual division of labor in the marketplace is perforce accompanied by a similar breakdown in marital roles, endangering marriage ties but also opening possibilities of mutual moves to greater role symmetry. Advocating support for such a move would mean that social institutions, including the workplace, would "be transformed so as to make this a reality, so that individuals would no longer be penalized in the economy for having active commitments to their families" (Matthei 1982, 328).

A further creative perspective on integration and gender roles is provided by theorists espousing recognition and appreciation of female values. Carol Gilligan (1982) posits that a model of women's development prizes attachment, concern with caring for others, and a context of interdependency. Accordingly, women seek to reconcile, to fuse love and work, in essence, to create an integrated model. In contrast, the long prevailing male model of human development has valued individuation, separation, a cutting of ties to others. These qualities are tangibly expressed in a work world which rewards them and which inherently discriminates against women possessing an alternative set of values. Thus, men successfully progress through a work world attuned to their values, emphasizing individuality, competitiveness, and separation from encumbering relationships. Women, by contrast, inevitably conflict with a work world which dishonors and disparages values of interconnectedness and nurturance. The reality of this value conflict is plainly echoed in work research detailing obstacles to integration, an obvious result of a workplace devoted to segregation. Although women's entry into the work force compelled a refocus of research inquiry toward fusion rather than breach, such research has not yet moved far beyond the detailing of strains, impediments, and difficulties. Ironically, most social science research is still guided by the prevailing logical positivist paradigm, criticized by feminists for being too reflective of male thinking. Only infrequently are feminist research strategies applied to the issue of female work experience, despite Gilligan's understated suggestion that "among the most pressing items on the agenda for research on adult development is the need to delineate in women's *own terms* (emphasis hers) the experience of their adult life (including) . . . the effects of these differences in marriage, family, and work relationships" (Gilligan 1982, 173).

LINK: FAMILY STRATEGY

> I don't make my family fit my work—I make my
> work fit my family. (A home working mother)

> The point is simply that compared with men the
> great majority of working women over the last
> century and a half have generally shaped their
> work around their family while, equally clearly,
> men have shaped their family life around their
> work. (Degler 1980, 434)

History contributes a valuable unifying theme to the fragmented pieces of information regarding family-work integration. That crucial missing link is family strategy, the concept that families "made choices and established priorities when responding to external pressures and internal needs" (Hareven 1984, 163). Historical investigators of work and family relationships maintain that families played a more activist role in constructing work patterns than they are generally credited with. Counter to more recent trends in social science which picture the family as an outcome variable of prevailing, powerful economic forces, these historical investigators outline convincing patterns of work choices determined by family life stage needs. Such research does not pretend that families make work choices independent of the larger economic framework, but does support the idea that families, given their personal constraints, make explicit choices of work strategy which most suitably meet family needs. Presuming connection rather than separation between work and family lives, the new social historians have illuminated the family context of work by deliberately highlighting familial work cultures long neglected by labor historians. Tilly and Scott (1978) examined historical patterns of women's work in France and England, contending that married women's work roles were plainly shaped by family needs as women chose occupations, work schedules and life cycle employment which most suitably responded to those needs. Hareven (1975, 1982) delineated numerous ways in which textile mill workers maintained familial networks which socialized for jobs, mediated employer demands, hired and placed workers, and in general demonstrated "resourcefulness and initiative in workers' responses to the pressures of efficiency and to the hazards of industrial life" (Hareven 1975, 249). Similarly, McGaw (1979) found that nineteenth-century married women workers in western Massachusetts chose paper mill work in preference to higher paying textile mill work for the greater flexibility and autonomy to fulfill family needs it offered them. Branca (1975) noted women's work patterns which indicated a strong preference for work arrangements most flexible for responding to family needs (such as domestic manufacture or home work), unique patterns often ignored by labor scholars because they did not occur in the same conventional organized factory settings as did men's work. A host of other historical studies of women's work repeatedly identify marital status as a crucial indicator of varying work patterns and arrangements over the life span.

Convincing though much of the historical evidence may be, contemporary social science has not readily incorporated the concept of family strategy into research inquiries on work and family. Logically, employing family strategy is entirely consistent with efforts to balance, juggle, or attain some harmony between work and family needs; negotiating changes and making choices are compatible, present-day expressions of an historically-derived concept.

Unfortunately, the concept of family strategy is not well suited to current research methods in social science. The implication of an activist family, choosing and implementing alternatives, is foreign to a research philosophy which assumes families to be dependent variables, molded by broader social and economic forces. A simple example is the vast preponderance of research describing unidirectional effects of maternal employment on children contrasted with the comparatively puny number of studies looking at children's effects on their mother's employment. Second, social science is primarily attuned to large scale survey, seeking out gross categorical variables (for example, the employed mother, child outcomes) a stance Kanter criticizes as a "quantitative emphasis on states and rates—or statics and snapshots" (1977, 20). Relatively little attention goes to how families perceive their work, conscious strategies they employ to reconcile work and family demands, and the considerations they weigh in achieving balance. Although it is within these "mediating variables" (Bronfenbrenner and Crouter 1982) or "intervening links" (Kanter 1977) that family strategy can be explored, the current prevailing research paradigm curbs such exploration. The few researchers who have creatively moved around this stumbling block to look individually at families' interaction with work have typically employed nonmainstream, alternative methodologies not favored by the social science establishment.

Thus restricted by both philosophy and methodology, social science has failed to consider some of the exciting contemporary possibilities raised by the historical concept of family strategy. Juggling and balancing are active, not passive behaviors, implying a rich variety of actions, choices, defeats, and rearrangements involving several people. Questions historians would like answered can best be handled by contemporary investigators:

> How did families plan their lives, particularly under conditions of adversity and rapid social change? What kinds of strategies did they follow in their adaptation to changing conditions over their life course and over historical time? How did family members juggle multiple roles and obliga-

tions as children, parents, members of a kinship network, and workers? How were individual careers synchronized with collective family ones? How were decisions made within the family? (Hareven 1984, 163)

Although shying away from family strategy as an articulated concept, social science has continued to generate useful piecemeal data which implicitly concedes strategy's existence. Disparate sources substantiate that families do indeed employ strategy, although the exact dynamics of such strategizing are masked. Examples include surveys indicating that women often make dramatic adjustments in their work life to respond to children's presence. Consistently, studies demonstrate married women's preference for part-time work, and other related forms of work life flexibility. A recent Gallup survey reported that an impressive 69 percent of working mothers would prefer flexible hour arrangements, including 12 percent who would prefer home-based work which they presumably view as supporting such flexibility. A related strategy question corroborated women's responses to family needs by asking working mothers, "Since having children, have you done any of the following?" Responding, women said that they quit work 28 percent, changed jobs or hours to spend more time with family 43 percent, and/or cut back on career goals 35 percent ("How Women View Work, Motherhood and Feminism" 1986). Unfortunately such survey research leaves us with little understanding of motivations and mechanisms involved in making such choices.

Research in a more academic vein has long tacitly sup ported the concept of strategy in its examination of the fertile area of dual role conflict. Fairly regularly and predictably, women with children differ from unmarried and/or childless women workers on a number of measures. Women with children are more likely to work fewer hours per week, to interrupt their work histories or otherwise alter their work patterns, to work geographically closer to home, and to experience greater stress on a variety of measures relating work and family lives. The work patterns of women with children are characterized by remarkable diversity, while women without children more closely approximately male work models (although voluntary childlessness may be a unique women's response to career demands). There appears to be no single, identifiable pattern of reconciling home and work lives among women with children except that it diverges from the male model. The diversity with which contemporary women respond to work and family needs testifies to the presence of family strategy. Further microlevel investigation will divulge some of the mechanisms by which families strategize.

LINK: THE PESSIMISTS

Finally, countering this rather diffuse sense of integration and the intuitive feel that it is a desirable goal are contemporary observers who scoff at the likelihood of such balance ever emerging. Arguing that work-family integration may be an unattainable dream in late twentieth-century America, they marshal persuasive statistical, anecdotal, and sociological data to support their position. The precarious vulnerability of late twentieth-century family life makes strategizing impermanent, assuring that large numbers of women and children are susceptible to economic insecurity. Single, femaleheaded households represent one of the 1980s fastest-growing poverty populations as children replace the elderly as the most numerous, age-identified segment of the poor. Some of this depressing growth represents women's longheld economic inequity in the labor market and their marginal earnings. Profound transformations in American family life account for more of the blame as ascending divorce rates have pushed women with their children into poverty. A recent study by Weitzman (1985) painfully demonstrated the consequences of divorce law liberalization for women and children, describing how the standard of living for divorced women and their children fell by 73 percent while the ex-husband's rose by 42 percent. Since mothers still typically receive custody of children, and the majority of absent fathers contribute nothing to their children's financial welfare, it is not difficult to see how women and children fall into poverty, or at least, greatly reduced circumstances. Projections currently indicate that at least 20 percent of all children live with a single (usually female) parent, and that probably 50 percent of children born in the 1980s will live in a one-parent (usually female) household. These sobering statistics, combined with a total lack of governmental support for families struggling in such positions, make integration a joke. Balancing becomes not a choice of the best options for fulfillment but instead a grim battle with reality. As yet, we have little sense of how single-parent households perceive the balancing act.

Even for families with more resources to draw upon, balancing can be an exhausting undertaking. Assembling an impressive array of personal and sociological testimony, Sylvia Ann Hewlett (1986) concluded that integration is impossible given the total lack of social support for working families in the United States. In glaring contrast to many European countries which promote family support policies, the United States offers no such option. Symptomatic of the historical American disregard for the lives of children, United States social policy toward children is at best non-existent and perhaps more accurately, unsympathetic. Parents seeking to enrich family life while maintaining productivity as workers receive no assistance, no governmental support for parental leave for birth or disability of a child, no encouragement of flexible work patterns which might allow them to reconcile competing needs, no financial support for child rearing, no meaningful economic support for increased and improved day care services. Hewlett's arguments provide a broader perspective to the finding of strains between working and parenting reported in academic studies.

Other pessimists point to cultural contradictions between working and parenting which construct impossible barriers to reconciliation. Hunt and Hunt (1982) maintain that people choosing to have families will become ghettoized and precluded from pursuing serious careers since employers will prefer childfree persons far more amenable to corporate demands for time and energy. In effect, "those who emphasize family life will gravitate toward greater role symmetry which will preclude availability for the most competitive, demanding, and often rewarding careers" (Hunt and Hunt 1982, 503). Certainly their pessimism may be well founded, particularly for women. Women choosing to hold down serious careers are less likely to be married and far more likely to be childless than the population of all women workers.

Degler (1980) argues that traditional family values collide with women's modern efforts to enter the work force on an equal footing with men. Women's continued linkage of work and family lives expresses values which are anti-individualistic and, by definition, unsuitable to success in the work-a-day world. In effect, concerning oneself with integration is a weakness, a disadvantage in a career world still implicitly prizing the old assumptions of segregated and self-less devotion to work. Barring a radical restructuring of the work world and/or men's immediate rush to assume household labor equally, neither of which is in the offing, Degler shares the Hunts' pessimistic view that integrators will be the work world's inferiors. Role symmetry is an illusion in a real world where one may not balance but instead must choose between work or family, period. What Degler describes as the resulting inevitable tension, or "woman's dilemma," remains unrelieved.

LINKING HOME WORK AND INTEGRATION

> Currently, families and individuals attempting to combine family and work have to rely too often on *ad hoc* individual rather than institutionalized collective solutions (Chow and Berheide 1988, 27)

> I've worked in a few mills where, you know, there were nice people to work for and all the rest—it was as pleasant a job as I could get. But it's certainly not pleasant punching a time clock. (A home-working mother)

> I worked in the shoeshop 8 years and 5 months in all. . . . And I knew I couldn't leave my kids. I cried every morning. (A home-working mother)

In late twentieth-century America, individual families retain the responsibility for redressing work-family imbalances. Greater symmetry between work and family life continues to be more an ideal than a common practice, undermined by the failure of employers and government policy to initiate widespread significant reforms which would make integration concrete and accessible. Despite tentative movement toward such a goal by some employers, some families, and some pieces of government policy, these efforts are fragmentary and often idiosyncratic. Sometimes they even appear contradictory. Families facing an unsympathetic response to their desire to create a healthier, mutual work-family interaction make the best arrangements they can. These arrangements may make sense on an individual, microsystem level but may be less attractive on a collective macrolevel. The outcry over home work and acrimonious debate over its value as a tool of accommodation or exploitation offers one such example. On the one hand, the female worker who wants to be home with her young children might view home work as a feasible alternative. So might the male looking for a reasonable income in a chronically underemployed rural economy. These people will filter their perceptions of home work through their own needs. The macrolevel historian, by contrast, doing his/her own filtering, might focus on the economic injustice or gender role ramifications of home work.

The following study, while not ignoring the concerns of macrosystem analysts, centers on the perspectives of families themselves. It aligns itself with their viewpoint to explore the daily reality of what happens when work and home again reunite in shared space. It charts the perceptions and involvement of all family members in an effort to understand how home work engages the entire family system. It recognizes that home work may indeed be an ad hoc response by individual families to a work system generally unsympathetic to work-family connections and not an ideal form of a collective or institutional response. Nonetheless, families' alternative arrangements deserve examination for the information they give us about individual initiative, family strengths and weaknesses, and the visions of work-family connections which some people hold. No claim is made that these families represent all home workers or that their experiences duplicate those of illegal immigrant seamstresses in New York City or electronics assemblers in the Southwest. We know enough from research to understand that race, class, and gender dramatically alter family experiences and outcomes. Rather, the families here demonstrate concretely one example of response to work-family integration—sharing work and family space. An intensive look at the consequences of that choice enhances our understanding of how some families seek to concretize links between work and family and raises questions we might explore with other families making the same effort. Finally, by scrutinizing how these families encounter home work as a tool for integrating, we can inject more of a needed microperspective into debate over the issue. It is this microlevel perspective of how families experience home work that infuses this study.

Chapter 2

Understanding Home Work Through Time and Space

The home has been the family shelter through the centuries. To prevent the distortion of its social function through use by profit-making industries is the responsibility of society. (U.S. Department of Labor, Women's Bureau, "Industrial Homework in Rhode Island," Bulletin No. 135, 1935)

The complex task remaining is to find a path that allows for an integration of the commitment to work and the commitment to the family. For each woman there is the arduous search to find a creative solution.

One way is via the homebased business. Many women have found this ideally suited to their requirements. . . . The central issues of work and love can be met in a setting conducive to both. (Lasker 1983, 20)

That home work does not exist in a vacuum is manifest in the contrasting comments above, one deploring work in the home, the other endorsing it. Not since the eighteenth century has home work been a neutral term, a mere descriptor of a physical fact. The removal of work from the home in the late eighteenth and early nineteenth centuries accomplished far more than a simple relocating of workspace. Profound changes in the nature of men's and women's work roles accompanied and flowed from a relatively innocuous change in workspace siting, imputing to home work a value-laden charge. For the first time, home work became a women's work style, intimately intertwined with women's fulfillment of gender-role expectations. Positioned on the ideological battlefield, home work aroused the fierce antipathy and passionate defense reflected in the opening quotes, a combat still taking place in a remarkably enduring contest. The Reagan administration's successful effort to remove remaining prohibitions on home work exemplifies this continuing barrage. After a fifty-year ban on home work in the knitted outerwear industry was lifted in 1985 by the Reagan administration, the home work argument centered, often furiously, on remaining prohibitions in six industries: women's apparel, jewelry, buttons and buckles, handkerchiefs, embroidery, and glove manufacture. Conservatives argue that home work should rightly be allowed as an expression of free enterprise, using shibboleths such as "constitutional right to work" and "work ethic" as key phrases supporting their argument; opponents employ words like "sweatshops," "exploited immigrants," and "substandard wages and working conditions" in arguing their cause. One reporter describes this continuing controversy as a replay of an ongoing ideological battle, positioning "the Administration's advocacy of free enterprise against defenders of New Deal laws that prohibit the exploitation of workers" (Noble 1986, A8). Curiously, few writers explore beyond these obvious ideological overtones to probe more extensively the fundamental issue characterizing home work, namely that it is primarily women's work. It is women who are the home workers in the industries under discussion, and it is women who have traditionally created and maintained home work in a special relationship which lies at the root of contemporary argument. Historical evolution of home work reminds us of this very special gender linkage which demands that we consider gender an important category of analysis.

Underlying and sustaining the durability of the home work controversy, of course, are the quite divergent opinions about gender role behavior implicit in the varying stances.

Women's proper work and family roles, perennially the focus of ideological strife, receive heightened and often conflicted play in the home work setting. Were women forced into home work by a sexist society, or did they choose it as a strategy for integrating? Should women be permitted routinely to earn wages within the home or should the home be a private haven uncontaminated by the corruption of the industrialized world? Is home work exploitive of women, or does it benefit them in any way? What about perceptions of the home workers themselves? What consequences for family life did home work portend? What did home work say about the roles of men and women in nineteenth- and twentieth-century America? Tracing home work's historical evolution is a necessary prerequisite to understanding its place in late twentieth-century America, entwined as contemporary home work is with historical precedent. These links remain visible today in the Reagan administration's effort to overturn home work bans in certain industries in order to unleash the forces of free enterprise among women and, perhaps correspondingly, keep them in their homes where they belong. Opposing removal of home work bans are labor unions with their own interests to defend. In the middle are home workers themselves who are infrequently consulted about their own perceptions of the battle. The origins of this rather confusing mishmash of gender role links to home work lie in history, as the current argument echoes longstanding disputes.

Reviewing home work's historical origins underscores the links to current preoccupation with integrating and also points out useful clues to employ in designing research. Historians' deliberate tracing of the connections between work and family augments the relatively scarce framework provided by social science. Finally, historical work stimulates critical questions regarding the nature of time, meaning of gender role, degree of family involvement and integration of work and family in home-working families.

Initially and importantly, historians underline a concept virtually unemployed by contemporary researchers: the pervasive significance of space in investigating work-family relationships. Contemporary social scientists share several tacit assumptions about space and time as related to work-family issues. Foremost among them is the physical separation of work and family space; except for farm families, the literature ignores the specific relationship of workspace and family consequences. Implicitly, the spatial metaphor of separation has been transformed into a psychological one, the same assumption of segregation of work and family lives which so long bolstered most research. Historical writing on the topic of workspace and family life, however, suggests that closer attention is needed to this heretofore unquestioned assumption. The widespread prevalence of subsistence farms in the eighteenth century and the virtue and necessity of producing the household's own cloth, food, and other items of consumption in the absence of factories led to joint participation in the family household economy for most rural and small town residents. The American Revolution and aftermath accentuated the need for independent self-sufficience as a new economy was built, free of reliance on England. Whether shared work and family space occurred in a farm setting, in an artisan's shop, or in the late eighteenth century as part of household manufacture-for-sale, which later gave way to the putting-out system, this sharing of work and family space created special consequences for family members. An ideological gender division of labor undoubtedly existed but it may have been softened by recognition of economic interdependence:

> the economic and productive interdependence of all family members diluted the meaning of women's economic status. Women depended on men to buy and work land and produce grain, but men had no bread without women baking it. Women's economic dependency was one strand of a web of interdependence of men's and women's typical work. (Cott 1977, 22)

Thus, though women and men assumed sex-appropriate tasks in theory, the mutuality of their endeavor complemented one another's role. Just how unbridgeable the gap between the sexes' duties was in truth remains unknown and historians disagree over the extent of gender-role flexibility in late eighteenth-century America. However, studies of mid-twentieth-century farm families who also share space (Boulding 1980; Vanek 1980) disclose far more mutual task involvement and joint decision making than might be expected in ostensibly traditional families; it is not unreasonable to expect that a similar gap between ideology and practice might have existed for colonial families sharing work space. Cott implies such joint participation, stating that "the expansion of nonagricultural occupations drew men and grown children away from the household, abbreviating their presence in the family and their roles in childrearing" (Cott 1977, 49). Certainly it appears from several sources that men were far more active in parenting than they subsequently became, principally because of a change in the notion of parenting. At the time when work and family space were shared, serving as an economic role model and socializing children for economic functions was a major parental job. Logically, parents included their children in household routines as an important learning task crucial to all their economic futures. Thus children, incidentally present in the workplace, probably participated in joint economic undertakings in whatever age-appropriate ways they could, undertakings in which the father figured prominently. Correspondingly, less emphasis was placed on the emotional aspects of parenting, and mothering was not the emotionally-charged concept it later became. In all likelihood, then, shared workspace implied some degree of shared parenting. Despite the concept of sex-appropriate tasks, parenting was not the sole responsibility of women—that came later in the nineteenth century. Instead, it appears that parenting was an activity shared by both parents and by outsiders as well—other family members, households to which children were apprenticed, and other farm homes where children were informally fostered—all resulting from children's importance and potential as economic producers in the joint family-work household.

Some contemporary theorists assert hopefully that shared home and work space will lead once more to a breakdown of rigidity in the sex/gender division of labor, assuming that the mutual intrusion of home and work space inevitably result in less stereotyping. Some feminists suggest that more work-at-home opportunities will lead to this happy outcome (Boneparth and Stoper 1983), a view shared by others such as Toffler (1980) who maintain that joint work-family space makes rigid gender boundaries impossible. History can offer no definitive conclusions on this topic, but it does suggest that life may have been quite different when work and family space were shared. At the very least, it may have been more difficult to fall back on social notions of appropriate behavior when confronted with a particular need in the intimacy of one's family. Shared space may have fostered the non-differentiation of sex roles which are a necessary ingredient of a symmetrical family.

As a changing economy created and forced work opportunities outside of the home in the early nineteenth century, work and family space diverged. The net effects of the separation of home and work were profound, far exceeding the simple physical fact of location. Separation eliminated any potential sharing of traditional sex role duties which may have characterized shared space families. The consequent increased privacy of the home afforded by the removal of work activities resulted in isolation for women as men entered and dominated the public sphere, relegating women to the private sphere. Left in the home with children and household duties (women's traditional responsibilities), female involvement with domestic matters increased, especially in child care as the ideal of the nurturing mother gained ascendancy. This public male/private female distinction intensified during the mid-nineteenth century to produce the cult of domesticity which rigidly and narrowly prescribed women's appropriate sphere. For the first time, women were cut off from overt economic productivity, an activity now considered rightly and properly the preserve of men. In its place, women were allocated a vastly exaggerated domestic role which confined them to housewifely matters. A principal component of this new role was mothering, heretofore a relatively non-pressured, casual, and shared activity. Now only a good mother could properly nurture tender young children who could flourish only with her full-time devotion. The glorification of the mothering role (and the corresponding devaluation of the fathering role) was one of the prime consequences of the removal of work from the home; shared economic productivity and shared parenting became physically and emotionally impossible. This divergence between men's and women's roles closely paralleled the separation of work from the home.

The divergence between men's and women's work was observed not only in space, as critical as space was to formulating the setting. Time also became a distinguishing criterion for the nature of work. For men entering the modernizing public workplace, time was redefined; no longer irregular, seasonal, subject to personal or natural rhythms, it became routinized, standardized, and allocated into work units governed by mechanical timepieces, a relatively recent invention essential to the industrialized workplace. This transformation of time from premodern task orientation to modern, disciplined time orientation was described by E. P. Thompson (1967) who noted one of its outcomes, "a clear demarcation between 'work' and 'life' " (p. 93).

Married women, by contrast, remained task oriented rather than assuming a time orientation:

> Household work, still the chief work of adult women, retained the irregularity, the responsiveness to immediate and natural demands, and the intermixture with social occasions common to preindustrial occupations. . . . Not the clock, but human need, regulated preparation of meals, sewing of garments, and tending of children. (Cott 1977, 60)

Married women's work, then, developed in diverse directions from men's. In such a context, home work for pay represented a distinct advantage for married women whose families needed additional financial support in order to survive. Home work for married women was acceptable, swathed in the cloak of the household setting. Respectably, it sheltered women from entering the masculine sphere (also conveniently shielding men from their competition). Genteely, home work also extended women's natural sphere since home workers usually worked in female-appropriate endeavors: sewing, laundering, taking in boarders, and other suitably domestic undertakings. Women's control over home work meant that it could be subordinated to other pressing needs and thus accommodated into the task rather than time orientation, allowing women to fulfill properly their household responsibilities. The emergence of the distinctive putting out system in the early nineteenth century dovetailed manufacturers' needs for an expanded, flexible, often seasonal, and cheaper labor force with married women's needs to accommodate work and family demands. Conveniently, the wages were usually low enough to merely supplement the husband's income rather than challenge it, so as to avoid upsetting the so-called natural order. Though census figures do not reveal the extent of women's involvement in home work (such women's work was generally subordinated to the head of household's labor status and thus went unreported in censuses), there is little doubt that women were substantially participating in textiles, boot and shoe making, clothing, hat and accessory articles on a home work basis (Abbott 1910). These occupations were essentially outgrowths of women's traditional home occupations and as such provided continuity with what women had always done. Although some men, chiefly artisans, continued also to work at home, gender proved more a distinguishing feature of work experience than did common occupation.

Home work thus evolved into married women's work, acquiring distinctive characteristics linking it with women's proper roles. Tied to a context of family duties, home work was acceptable and flexible, permitting (or demanding) an early form of integration. Further, home work set married women on a divergent track from men's work experiences wherein women's encounters with space and time were profoundly different. It is no overstatement to say that the removal of work from the home set men's course toward the segregated ideal while women's steps were guided (or forcibly led) toward the integrated model.

Married women's link with home work marks another work divergence, this time between single and married women. Gradually, single women were entering the separate work place, working in textile mills, shoe factories, or other households as domestic labor. Single women, unencumbered by the need to integrate, developed work habits perhaps more analogous to men's, thus creating a threefold category of gender analysis regarding work: married women's work, single women's work, and men's work. This threefold categorization, a product of nineteenth-century work experience, still pertains quite accurately in contemporary research which regularly delineates differences among the work experiences of women with families (be they married or single parents), women without families (including single women and married women with no children) and men. This divergence not only between men's and women's work but also between single and married women's work is nicely illustrated in a comprehensive article on early shoemaking by Blewett (1983). In her article, Blewett depicted how home-working female shoebinders remained firmly tied to their family context, thus circumscribing their ability to organize as workers. Blewett's work reinforced the important distinction between married and single women in shoe work: single women went into the factory to work and eventually gained an identity as a worker while married women remained shoebinding at home, enmeshed in a family identity which precluded their developing identities as workers. Their family status infused their perception of work experience.

That married women remained tied to a family role which superseded their work role has been argued persuasively by other historians. McGaw's (1979) examination of work patterns among nineteenth-century women in western Massachusetts found that female heads of households were more likely to choose paper mill work over higher paying textile mill employment because the former allowed shorter, more flexibly scheduled workdays which presumably enabled them to attend to household responsibilities. Hareven (1982) found life cycle stages of work force participation among women millworkers, depending on family needs. In this light, married women's apparent preference for home work remained logical. Branca (1975) elaborated on this preference, noting that women's work has historically been ignored by labor historians because it did not occur in the same conventional, organized factory settings as men's work did. Instead, "women wanted to work in or near a family context, within the home where possible" (Branca, 1975, p. 146) and her subsequent analysis of work patterns indicated large numbers of uncounted women working in domestic manufacture. Rather than labeling such women as slaves to the traditional division of labor, Branca redefined such work as innovative and responsive to changing social and economic conditions. She maintains that such adaptations reflect not servitude but reconciliation, evidencing "women's distinctive ability to initiate changes in work roles even in traditional settings" (p. 129).

By the mid-nineteenth century, then, working at home became most closely associated with married women. It was single women who became mill operatives, teachers, and domestic workers—the other most common sources of employment for women at that time. This simple divergence in workspace location led to more far-reaching and disparate implications: single women's experience of work was probably more individualistic than married women's who submerged their consciousness into a family identity and worked in relative isolation from others. Consequently, married women were less likely to participate in any collective labor action than were single women and more inclined to couch their requests for wages in terms of family position (supplementing the husband's wage) rather than objective merit. Men were also more likely to view home-working married women through their family role rather than according them respect as workers; the wage work that such women performed was acceptable and compatible with women's roles as household supporters, adjuncts of more important men's work. Moreover, the continued location of married women's work in the home reinforced the prevailing stereotype of women's appropriate domestic sphere of duties, a notion which would have been directly challenged had women entered men's separate workplaces. Gender role expectations by now plainly pervaded the concept of home work.

By the turn of the twentieth century, home work had assumed some new characteristics not entirely discrepant with previous aspects. The earliest types of home work—outcomes of women's traditional home industry—in textiles, clothing, and shoes had been substantially absorbed and relocated to the factory. The logical associations with small farms and women's household production of "Cloth, Butter and Boarders" (Jensen 1980) as sources of income were gone, replaced by different kinds of work. Tedious, low paid hand work as part of a factory process replaced traditional household production; immigrants rather than the wives and daughters of farmers became the laborers, at least in urban areas. Now, home work involved jobs such as stringing beads, embroidering baby clothes, making lace, creating artificial flowers, sewing uppers on shoes and other similarly exacting tasks undertaken as one step in a factory process. At this point, home work became synonymous with sweatshop, and the exploitation of home workers roused the ire of reformers who finally succeeded in banning most types of home work by the 1930s. The crusading zeal of the reformers resulted in the politicization of home work as its abuses were disclosed and regulated. The outpouring of indignation about home work was reflected in U.S. Women's Bureau pamphlets such as "The Commercialization of the Home Through Industrial Home Work" (1935), "The Employment of Women in the Sewing Trades of Connecticut" (1935), "Industrial Home Work" (1930), and "Industrial Home Work in Rhode Island" (1935). Such condemnations effectively presented quantitative data about the existence of home work, particularly noting the tedium, low wages, and sometimes unsanitary nature of the home workplace, but left the home workers themselves without a voice. Whether these women shared any experiences of earlier home workers is almost impossible to discern. It does seem clear, however, that the outcry over violation of the home through income-producing activities reflects and extends the nineteenth-century mythology of the home as a private sphere, free of the taint of corruption of the male, public world.

Contemporary theorists, extending this argument, describe the precise mechanisms by which gender role expectations suffused and directed home work reform efforts. Boris (1985) labeled home work regulation as "the triumph of sacred motherhood," tracing how it reflected gender expectations that married women should be at home with children and that the home should be protected from corrupting influences. Of course, while boxing in and protecting sacred motherhood, protective legislation also ensured that women's labor would continue to be devalued, relegated to secondary wage earner status. For such critics, home work expresses perfectly the exploitation of women by an oppressive economic system.

Other theorists continue relating the theme of home work and exploitation. Johnson's (1982) study of Canadian industrial home seamstresses described the oppressive conditions under which her predominantly immigrant sample labored. Cultural expectations are personified by a system which continues to exploit women: "It (home work) exists today for the same reasons that supported it fifty and even 150 years ago. For workers—mainly women with young children—it is a way of combining household commitments with paid employment. For employers, it is a way of reducing overhead and keeping wages down" (Johnson 1982, 9). Similarly, Boris' (1987) interpretation of Vermont home knitters' struggle to gain legal acceptance outlined home work's persistent reliance on women's unpaid household labor and status as secondary wage earners, reinforcing women's economic (and political) inequality. Christensen's (1987) examination of home-based employment also cautioned against exploitation, concentrating in a familiar vein on women's efforts to reconcile family and income demands through working at home. These observers raise legitimate issues of pay, work standards, and gender role inequality particularly pertinent to the lives of home-working women. In making powerful arguments conceptualizing home work as an exploitative expression of a patriarchal economic system, they represent quite articulately the prevailing opinion about home work.

Such a macrosocial view may indeed be politically correct, while on the microsocial level the family may perceive things quite differently. Boris notes this tension between individual and system: "Although home work has been a strategy for individual women to cope with limited opportunities in the workplace, it has done so at the cost of reinforcing the subordinate position of women as a group in the economy and perhaps also in the family" (Boris 1987, 102). However, other equally committed feminists suggest that this nexus may not necessarily represent continued exploitation but may instead represent a tool for change (Boneparth and Stoper 1983). Working at home, they say, may create a setting for restructuring work for both women and men, one which permits both genders to equalize their roles, thus breaking with historical precedent.

Such an argument between historical tradition and futurist predictions underscores the importance of examining the actual experiences of home-working families. Ideological positioning aside, it is the mundane experiences of such families that best help us to understand circumstances under which home work may be an adaptive strategy healthy for families, or a continued tool of economic, patriarchal oppression. By attending to the voices and actions of individual families, we can get a sense of the specific factors affecting outcomes for home-workers.

When efforts are made to seek out the input of the home workers themselves, women's voices provide another perspective. Benson's (1979) analysis of raw data collected for the

U.S. Women's Bureau 1934 examination of the home lace industry in Rhode Island offers some continuities with home work's meaning for earlier generations of women. She found that these women, while not unconscious of low wages, felt that such home work provided them the opportunity to earn wages while integrating wage work with family duties; phenomenologically, "what is striking is the adaptability and flexibility of home work rather than its unambiguously oppressive quality" (Benson 1979, 21).

Shallcross braved the ire of reformers in her book on home work, acknowledging that "this volume is a challenge to the rigid notions which now prevail" (Shallcross 1940, xiii). Most relevant is her description of reasons for undertaking home work, based on the perceptions of home workers themselves. It is quoted at length because of its applicability to the present study:

> It may be said here that homeworkers have a definite preference for working at home, which makes them compute real wages from homework in a manner which monetary wages would not seem to justify. This preference for working at home is based on several factors which are primarily social. First, the desire for some remunerative work of a type which complements the unpredictable demands of housework leads many married women to choose homework rather than factory work. This reason, while being an economic one, is also a social one when it indicates that housework and family take precedence over homework. Second, the impossibility of working in a factory because of some form of incapacitation leads to a desire to do homework. This reason is both an economic and a social one inasmuch as the desire to work at home frequently arises from both an economic need and a need to engage in purposeful activity. The therapeutic value of homework for those who are incapacitated has received very little attention in the literature on homework. . . .
>
> Even when ability or family responsibility does not close factory opportunities, some workers prefer homework to the strains of factory work. Thus, the third social reason why homework exists is that many women prefer homework because of its lack of supervision and freedom from the fatigue factors of speed, complexity and noise associated with factory life. Every inspector who, over a period of years, has vis-

ited different types of homeworkers finds this reason for doing homework a common one. Homeworkers generally recognize the benefit of being able to work under circumstances which are not directly supervised. The economic pressure to work at home may be as great as that to work in the factory, but the strain which may result from direct supervision is removed. . . .

The fourth reason why homework is preferable to factory work for some workers is explained only by an analysis of the mores of certain nationality groups. Nationality reasons have played a very important role with both Italian and Jewish homeworkers, who make up the first and second largest national groups among licensed homeworkers in New York City. (p. 26–27)

Reports such as these indicate that interpreting home work requires inclusion of both extrinsic and intrinsic factors. Questions of wage rates, piece work, work conditions and workday length have long been legitimate concerns of labor historians and social reformers. The amassing of quantitative data on these aspects of work remains an important part of the interpretation of work experience. Such an interpretation is incomplete, however, without listening to the voices of the workers themselves. Such a microsocial focus, generally missing from home work literature, is the focus of this study.

Summing up, history lends several valuable lessons to social science in undertaking a study of home work. One is that "home work" is a value laden term, not just a description of shared work and home space. The evolution of home work has involved ideological changes mirroring societal needs and conceptions. It has undoubtedly served as a focus of demarcation between men's work and women's work experiences, providing vastly disparate perspectives on work and family. Historical data strongly indicate the intertwining of women's family motivations and home work, though on the perceptions and daily experiences of these women we are less informed. Most researchers have underscored the exploitive nature of home work, emphasizing it as a manifestation of an unjust, sexist and/or capitalist society. An alternative view is volunteered by social historians who suggest that home work may have been a feasible strategy for integrating, an indication not of women's weakness but of a unique strength to understand what is truly important and to arrange their lives accordingly. Which perspective reveals the truth is in itself a matter of current controversy among historians, some of whom maintain that women's inequality in the labor force results from historical discrimination versus others who argue that it emanates from women's deliberate choices of alternative work arrangements.

Such historical research sets the stage for a contemporary investigation of women's home work relative to child care, household labor, structure and nature of the workday, and gender role expectations. It strongly implicates the role of space in affecting profoundly the enactment of work and family roles, and suggests that experiences of time may be distinct as well. By attending to variations in work patterns rather than uniformities, it reminds social science about diversity and the value of appreciating complexity. Finally, new social historians' insistence on examining the family context of work decisions, documented through their research, provides an incentive for social scientists to leave behind the assumed primacy of work over family relationships to study interrelationships instead.

In response to the valuable guideposts provided by historians, social scientists can offer history some service as well. Primarily, historians have lacked data on actual family settings, the mechanics whereby their theories might operate. An examination of such microlevel experiences can augment, confirm, or deny historical suppositions about the family context of work. Precise information about the nature of the home worker's day, allocation of labor within the household, expressed motivations for undertaking home work, working conditions, children's involvement, comparative experiences of male and female home workers, and how time and space are utilized in work and family life all serve as grist for analyzing the continuity of present-day home work with its antecedents. Such an interplay of historical and contemporary data gathering complements each discipline.

Chapter 3

Defining and Measuring Integration

We shall understand families when we understand how they manage the commonplace, that is, how they conduct themselves and interact in the familiar surroundings of their own household. (Kantor and Lehr 1975, ix)

From an observation of a home-working family (the father, Todd, is working on business matters at a desk in the gallery of his home):

10:35: Todd takes watercolor off wall, places it against door to outdoors, snaps a Polaroid. Nate (4M) is still working quietly on floor with Legos. Baby sister starts grabbing at Nate's Legos, mother suggests using Pa's desk, "unless you (Pa) need it." Todd says he's working but Nate can have room. He clears off front of desk (Sheraton table); Nate runs out and returns with a Windsor high chair which he places at table opposite father to play. Todd starts typing at electric typewriter; sister runs over to corner to ride on rocking horse; Nate and Dad at table working (Legos and typing).

CHOOSING STRATEGY

How home-working families manage the commonplace constitutes the core of this study. Examining families in their familiar surroundings seems like a logical first step in understanding their experiences of integrating. By carefully using families' own words and experiences, the researcher grounds herself in their definitions rather than imposing her own definition on an admittedly imprecise concept. The research task, then, appears simple: to observe families in their everyday setting, to garner input from all family members, and to sift through the information obtained to generate reasonable conclusions. Logically, one chooses a research strategy supporting this aim.

Unfortunately, sensible as such an approach might seem, it does not represent prevailing research methodology in social science. Contemporary research, dominated by a logical positivist paradigm, seeks to isolate, control, and predict discrete variables. In emulating the hard sciences, social scientists typically rely on quantitative methods to test differences between comparable groups, aiming at maximum generalizability over large numbers of subjects. Pragmatically, this means that researchers, straining to be objective, only rarely come in direct contact with their subjects, infrequently solicit the subjects' own viewpoints or perceptions, and avoid real-life settings in favor of the more classic, experimentally controlled conditions of the laboratory. The resulting "quantitative emphasis on states and rates—or statics and snapshots" (Kanter 1977, 20) can indeed provide useful information on single variables but is less suited to explore complex interactions occurring over time.

This prevailing research approach has been severely criticized for both its basic assumptions and methods by researchers who claim it represents only one way of looking at truth. Chief among critics' complaints is that overreliance on quantitative methods produces research which denies social context, glorifies the generality while disregarding important diversity in human life, and focuses only on narrow aspects of life rather than the complexity of interrelationship which more accurately characterizes the human condition. Further, feminist researchers particularly criticize this research paradigm for ignoring women's life and work experiences, maintaining that it best measures and perpetuates a male-oriented outlook on human life. Two feminist researchers of family life succinctly summarize some of the major contrasts between logical positivism and a countervailing collection of theories loosely defined as qualitative research:

Agentic scholars separate, order, quantify, manipulate, control, and reduce, consistent with abstract aims and the goal of generalization. Communal scholars integrate, search for patterns, accept dualities and complexity, reach out to participants, and listen to and report what people have to say about their lives. (Walker and Thompson 1984, 546)

This latter approach, contradictory to the way most research is currently conducted, fits more consonantly with a study of work and family life. Issues likely to be associated with integration—consideration of multiple viewpoints, appreciation of the context in which it occurs, and understanding of the diversity with which individuals and families construct their alternatives—cannot be readily separated, isolated, and assigned numerical weights. According to this perspective, it is no coincidence that integration has never been a topic of research; for many years, the standard quantitative methodology nicely complemented the view that work was a man's world, segregated from other compartments of human life. When work and family were dichotomous, with interactive connections denied or ignored, it was easier to isolate and manipulate variables pertaining solely to the worker. The few studies that did seek out connections usually focused solely on the worker, soliciting his reactions but almost never approaching spouses and certainly never children for any multiple perspectives. Rarely was a worker observed in both work and family settings. Thus, the prevailing methods in social science research reinforced prevailing social expectations about men's work.

This relationship was challenged by the rise of feminism and the influx of women into the workplace. As women agitated for recognition of the connections between working and loving, social science had to readjust its perspective to attend to the flow of work-family interaction. Researchers who moved around the stumbling blocks of unsuitable methods to look individually at families' interaction with work utilized alternative paradigms which incorporated participants' viewpoints, embraced multiple perspectives, examined context, and took place in natural settings—that is, homes and workplaces. Ironically and appropriately, the study of integration demands a strategy which itself integrates both methods and perspectives. These new strategies are still being developed, but this study employs several of their suggested features in an effort to adhere faithfully to the complexity of the issue under investigation. As we move from the "work effects on family" model to a truly interactive examination, new and more appropriate research strategies will emerge.

Home-working families offer an unusual opportunity to translate alternative research concepts into practical strategy. Relatively unresearched, they provide a fresh source of information about how work and family life may fit together without prematurely narrowing potential insights. Exploring details of their daily lives meets several important criteria of feminist family research as outlined by Walker and Thompson: recognition of the importance of sociohistorical context; gender and position as categories of analysis; emphasis on intragroup heterogeneity; recognition of complexity; research that is useful; emphasis on pluralism; and rejection of hierarchy in the research process (1984, 548–553). In this view, to define integration required that it be studied through the eyes of participants without prior assumptions, using their words and behaviors rather than superimposing a standardized single instrument. Measuring integration demanded using several methods capable of capturing a complex setting from multiple points of view—children's, worker's, and spouse's. At all times, definitions and measurements of integration were tied to the participants' own perceptions and behaviors rather than reflecting the researcher's reality.

These alternative research guidelines were joined with a more traditional systems approach to family study. Essentially, systems theorists maintain that "families are relatively 'open' systems; that is, they are embedded in a complex social structure and are connected to other social institutions in a variety of ways" (Piotrkowski 1978, 4). Acknowledging rather than denying connections between work and family life provides a useful starting point for evaluating research strategies. However, despite the enthusiasm which exists for both systems theory and the broader ecological approach as vehicles for appreciating the interaction of two such compelling spheres of human life, the inherent complexity of such an approach has produced discouraging results. Such design has only infrequently been applied to work-family research (Schulenberg, Vondracek, and Crouter 1984). Subjects of study in one context (for example, work) are almost never observed in their other context (family). Most typically, family members are interviewed in one setting only and asked questions about the other. Further, as noted earlier, children are rarely included in such research despite their standing as family members.

Families working at home remedy some of these inherent difficulties. Their combined home and work space affords the opportunity to observe easily in both settings. The physical presence of spouses and children makes their input impossible to ignore. The interaction between work and family life is more concretely and efficiently viewed than in disparate settings. And, while each family is individual in its functioning, such families are free of potentially confounding extrinsic variables such as employer attitudes, commuting time, external work schedules, etc. These families' construction of work and family routines and interaction patterns also provide a natural setting for study rather than the artificiality of the laboratory. The critical importance of observing families in their own contexts—their own natural settings—is common to a systems perspective. Unfortunately, despite the value of naturalistic observation for the family researcher, it is infrequently used as a research strategy.

Other difficulties present themselves in attempting to employ alternative research strategies. Standardized instruments commonly used to measure work-related behaviors are generally inappropriate or inapplicable to home-working families. Further, measures of work behaviors or family interaction alone would not suffice to capture the mutuality implied by integrating both domains. Since input from all family members was sought, no one-instrument measure would be adequate to capture both the adult worker's point of view and that of her two-year-old daughter. A further refinement among children themselves was necessary: verbal children can respond to a special children's interview format but non-verbal children also influence their parent's work role. Their input was gained through observation.

Although interview can extract much valuable data, cautions against overreliance on interview have been raised by investigators questioning its accuracy (Weller and Luchterhand 1969), and its ability to capture the full picture of a system's functioning (Klein, Jorgensen, and Miller 1978). Accordingly, observation and quantitative measures of time allocation were also taken as a check on interview's reliability. As a further safeguard, interviews were obtained from all verbal family members rather than just the home worker. (Most studies of workers rely solely on input from the worker alone; rarely is direct data sought from other family members). This effort to collect data from several sources and to cross-check it is one method of verification or "triangulation" suggested by qualitative researchers (Guba 1981).

Reciprocity, another cornerstone of systems theory, is more elusive to capture. Methodologically, this requires attention to both work and family activities, some longitudinality, and repeated rather than single measures. It also demands consideration of phenomenology (families' own perceptions of their settings) in order to understand the nature of mutual family responsiveness. Families who agreed to participate in this study are uniquely suited for attempting to distill some sense of reciprocity: all potential worker and familial roles were open to examination in one unit. Further, each family's agreement to participate included repeated visits, whole family interviews and observations, and a unique opportunity to observe interplay of work and family activities. The next section on procedure describes how this complex strategy was put into practice.

PROCEDURE

Extracting a research strategy from such a melange of emphases on complexity, context, and plurality presented a challenge. Given the lack of substantial precedent for such a messy exploration, and the fact that "feminist scholars are in the process of creating feminist methodology; that is, we cannot identify any single approach as the feminist method" (Walker and Thompson 1984, 554) any choice of research strategy is an experiment in itself. Nonetheless, I devised the following procedure, endeavoring both to implement an alternative research strategy and to seek some coherent truth about home-working families. Although the identified prime participant was the home worker providing the ostensible rationale for the unique employment choice (fifteen of them), the full number of participants included the fifty-seven adults and children who contributed data. I employed the following methodology, combining qualitative and quantitative measures.

1. Semi-structured interview with adult family members: the interview, held jointly with both adult family members or individually where required by other constraints, consisted of two parts: a Demographic Data Sheet which gathered factual information, and a Family Work Interview which addressed home working more directly.

2. Naturalistic observation by the researcher of the work-family process: I observed each family twice, two hours per observation, on a typical workday. Field notes (literal observational accounts) were taken during each observation period.

3. Structured interviews with verbal children: I interviewed the twenty-four verbal children concerning their understanding of their parent's work.

4. Daily time logs: each time worker submitted two daily logs reflecting incidents of work and family interaction. I quantified these logs for number of interactions, amount of time, and nature. Such logkeeping provided a quantifiable check on information regarding time use obtained through interview and observation.

5. Analysis of historical data: to provide a link to larger sociohistorical context, the historical background of home work was researched. The results are reported in chapter 2.

Data gathering took place over six months (January through July 1984). All interviews and observation occurred in the participants' homes at times convenient to them. Befitting a systems approach, I analyzed data from interviews, observations, and logs to extract "themes" (Glaser and Strauss 1967) which paint a portrait of the individual, his/her family, and work. Charts and figures are presented to substantiate these themes, while interviews and observations are excerpted to provide a sense of the data upon which conclusions were constructed. All themes emerged from the data; that is, no preconceived categories existed prior to data collection. Instead, I examined all raw data to generate the participants' reality from it. Once themes emerged, they were cross-checked (triangulated) with other sources; that is, information emerging from the parents' interviews was compared with information from children's interviews, and/or observations, and/or logs and/or demographic information in an effort to substantiate conclusions.

In such a light, the results that follow conform to efforts to define and measure integration through the eyes of the home workers themselves. Drawing upon a number of sources, it offers some tangibility to an intuitively appealing image rooted in the daily, commonplace experiences of the families themselves. Rather than offering abstractions, the results reported here draw heavily on families' own words and daily activities to offer a practical model of integrating work and family life. Ultimately, conclusions drawn about home work as a suitable strategy are grounded not in abstract theory but in pragmatic application, underscoring feminist research orientation toward the socially useful rather than simply the empirically valuable.

THE PARTICIPANTS

Since definitions and measurements of integration emerged from the families themselves, their important contribution to the research process must be acknowledged. Generously, fifty-seven men, women, and children from home-working families contributed time and conscientious effort to this study. Through frank interviews, scrupulous time logs, and naturalistic observations, they reveal details of their lives. Gradually, a picture of an integrated work style appeared, drawn from their own thoughts, words, and actions. The small details of their daily lives illumined the connections between working and loving. On a theoretical level, they offered a testing ground for working out complex issues of methodology and constructing a model of integrating; on a pragmatic level, they provided substance for other families interested in integrating work and family life to consider.

Qualitative researchers openly recognize and appreciate the significant contribution of families like those who cooperated in this study. Indeed, the relationship between qualitative researchers and cooperators represents a fundamental contrast between quantitative and qualitative research; quantitative researchers have "subjects" who are manipulated while qualitative researchers prefer to describe them as "participants" in a mutual learning endeavor. Plainly, the volume of learning generated by the cooperation of participants in this study elevates them far above the status of subjects. As their lives speak pointedly to a question crucial to the lives of many Americans, the insights they offer help fill a major void. The assistance of these fifty-seven men, women and children is gratefully acknowledged.

Characteristics of Participants

Fifteen home workers and their families participated in this study, a total of thirty adults and twenty-seven children. Since home work is so strongly linked with family structure, I chose a base of intact families with children to study. To meet the criteria for participation, all workers were in intact families in which there was at least one child under eighteen residing at home. All were residents of two rural counties in Maine.

Identifying and contacting potential participants presented special problems. Families working at home are usually self-selected and independent of membership in unions or associations relating to their employment; they can not be easily contacted through any group membership. (The dearth of studies of this group may reflect their inaccessibility to investigators). At the time of the study, the Bureau of Economic Analysis and Research of the Maine Department of Labor reported no statistics on home work, and no knowledge of home workers' number, gender, or occupations. The same research unit reported no statewide home work association to contact. The U.S. Census Bureau does offer rough parameters on number through a long form 1980 census question on work commuting patterns in which they projected 555 home workers in one of the Maine counties under study out of a labor force of 12,108. There is no further information available on actual number of hours worked, sex of home workers, income, nature of employment, etc.

Two previous studies I did with family day care providers and home shoe stitchers worked around the accessibility obstacle by utilizing snowball sample methods. Starting with an initial two names suggested by community informants, each interviewee was asked to name two other people they knew of who worked at home. This provided an adequate number of people to study and created a small pool of initial subjects for the present study. Snowball sampling (Herriott and Firestone 1983) can be utilized effectively when there is no claim to representiveness or randomness, and the sample can be checked against demographic data for comparison with the general population. It may also be an especially appropriate sampling technique in small rural communities where personalized knowledge of residents is common. An additional virtue is that snowball sampling takes sample control out of the researcher's hands and forces him or her to respond to the reality of the field. The sample in this study developed in diverse directions. Further, upon initiating the study, I had no knowledge of who would constitute the final pool of participants and thus could not readily preform categorizations into which I could force the data; on the contrary, I had to watch the emerging data very carefully in order to construct any disciplined abstractions.

Using this snowball method, seventeen families were ultimately contacted to ask their willingness to participate. Two families were unable to do so, principally because not all family members could agree to be interviewed and/or observed. The fifteen families who initially agreed to participate remained with the study throughout the several months of data collection; there were no dropouts.

The final sample reflected a wide range of occupation, class, and education, the principal demographic concerns of most researchers. The only remarkable characteristics were (1) the slightly greater number of women (9F, 6M) which may reflect simply the chance of the sampling method with a small group, or the greater propensity of women to work at home, and (2) the absence of very young people (ages eighteen to twenty-five) which may accurately reflect young people's notion that work occurs in conventional settings or that family motivations, especially the presence of young children, underlie the decision to work at home (subsequently borne out in results). Table 3–1 sets forth the principal demographic characteristics.

Table 3–1
Principal Demographic Characteristics of Home Workers (N=15)

Home Work Occupation	Sex	Age	Education (Years)
Day Care Provider	F	33	14
Knitter	F	38	17
Mechanic	M	40	14
Chef	M	42	15
Knitter	F	27	9
Knitter	F	27	12
Hairdresser	F	27	14
Knitter	F	50	12
Translator	F	45	20
Seamstress	F	38	14
Cabinetmaker	M	29	13
Veterinarian	M	37	20
Flytyer	M	37	16
Fine art dealer	M	31	16
Secretary	F	36	16

Occupationally, home workers varied in the nature of their work. Most were self-employed although the four knitters worked at home for a larger concern. Educationally, the most remarkable feature of this group lies in its diversity rather than uniformity. Education levels are slightly higher than the county medians of 12.5 years. One-third of the group holds a baccalaureate degree or higher, while two-thirds (nine participants) range from nine years of high school to some post-secondary (usually vocational) training. Education reported may be a function of this particular group or an indication that home work requires some additional skill beyond that of a general high school education.

The one characteristic common to all home workers was previous, out-of-the-home work experience. All fifteen had prior work histories which enabled them to compare home work with conventional employment. For seven of them, their home work occupation was similar or related to their previous employment while the remaining eight changed occupations to work at home. Table 3–2 sets forth the nature of these occupational changes.

A final set of demographic characteristics especially relevant to this study is current residence duration and home work occupation duration, which produced no obvious pat-

Table 3–2
Previous Occupations of Home Workers

Changed Occupations (N=8)	
Current	*Previous*
Knitter (3)	Millworker (3)
Mechanic	Truck driver
Hairdresser	Millworker
Knitter	Nurse's aide
Seamstress	Nurse
Secretary	Social service worker

Unchanged from previous occupation (N=7)
Day care provider
Translator
Cabinetmaker
Veterinarian
Flytyer
Fine art dealer
Chef

tern. Home workers had been performing their home-based employment for a range of one to thirteen years, while they had occupied their present residences for a range of four to twenty-seven years. Although two participants had purchased their homes explicitly because the homes were suited to their occupations, there was no consistent pattern among the other participants relating residence and home work duration.

All of the families had children, a condition of the study. Children's ages ranged from seven months to eighteen years, for a total of twenty-seven children averaging slightly fewer than two children per family. No family had more than three children currently residing at home, although one parent had raised fourteen children, only one of whom was still residing in the home. Children's age/sex breakdown appear in Table 3–3.

Perhaps the most remarkable feature about these families is their very ordinariness. Their occupations are not exotic, nor are their personal demographics widely divergent from most Americans. They do not represent a highly specialized work force or an elite segment of the population. While not representative in the quantitative researcher's strict defini-

Table 3–3
Children's Age and Sex in Home Worker Families

Preschool Age (0–6)	
Males	3
Females	8
School Age (7–12)	
Males	5
Females	8
Teenage (13–18)	
Males	1
Females	2

tion, their daily circumstances would look familiar to many Americans. All too often in the past, studies of work and family life have concentrated on individuals not typical of most workers' experiences: the dual-career professional couple, the executive woman, the academic couple. Even studies which peripherally mention working at home often feature the atypical, the man or woman with unusual resources. An example is a recent *Fortune* magazine study (Taylor 1986) of women MBA's who have chosen to opt out of the corporate world at rates far higher than their male counterparts. In so doing, many of these women, seeking greater family time, have chosen to work at home as independent consultants. Although their voices rightly should be heard, particularly as they underscore the appeal of integrating, such talented women have financial and educational resources greatly exceeding those of most women workers. The majority of American working women still cluster in the lower echelons of the pink, white, and blue collar worlds, lacking the resources available to women in management. Most women's options for alternative employment are far more restricted, and their strategies for balancing perhaps more challenging. Only by examining the experiences of a variety of workers at different levels can patterns emerge and commonalities be discussed. Certainly, working at home may offer quite a different context for the executive business consultant, married to a highly paid spouse, who utilizes supplementary child care, than the women whose only real option as described by one of the study participants, is "What would you rather do—cook, wash, and look after the kids (while working at home) or would you like to go in to the shoeshop? You have the choice."

For these families, then, the ordinariness of their lives is a virtue. They can speak plainly to the lives of far more American workers, and their experiences at making home work successful lend many concrete applications. The significance of their lives for examining integration lies not in superior or exotic resources but in the homely details of their daily lives. Only by examining those daily lives does the imagery of integrating achieve substance.

CONTEXT OF SAMPLE CHARACTERISTICS

Finally, in qualitative research, the study sample is inevitably linked to the context from which it emerges. Unlike quantitative research which searches for context-free generalizability in random sampling, qualitative researchers assume that "generalizations of the rationalistic variety are not possible because phenomena are intimately tied to the times and contexts in which they are found" (Guba 1981, 80). This is the same argument made by Bronfenbrenner (1979) in advocating that researchers pay more attention to ecological features affecting human interaction, though he cautions that naturalistic settings per se are no guarantee of ecological validity without seeking the participants' own perceptions of the situations. Thus, though the chief demographic characteristics of the participants have been delineated in the preceding section, it is also important to note some of the ecological factors which may affect their membership in the sample, and by extension, the "transferability" (Guba's (1981) term in preference to "generalizability") of the results.

Rural, rather than urban residence, contributes several potentially distinguishing features. According to several studies, rural residents are more likely to perform home-based work than urban dwellers. A study of home-based white collar workers revealed a disproportionate number of rural residents among them (Kraut and Grambsch 1987), a finding reinforced by home work publications directed toward people in non-urban areas, such as those issued by the USDA Extension Service. Both positive and negative reasons exist for this finding, several of which were suggested by participants in this study. One mundane but significant factor is the lack of zoning controls in the two rural counties involved in the study. Thus, barriers which might restrict the flow of individuals of particular occupations into home work in other geographic settings are negligible here. A second similar facilitating factor is the relatively low crime rate which does not put people in fear of opening publicly accessible businesses in their homes. Relative poverty is also somewhat of a virtue in encouraging home work: 1980 census data indicated Maine ranks forty-sixth in median household income and both counties represented in this sample had median incomes below the state's median. Low incomes, coupled with the unavailability of attractive jobs, enhances the appeal of self-employment and home work. As one participant stated:

> If you were working in Detroit making $12–$15 an hour, you could make a good argument for going and doing it. But when you're making the kind of money a lot of people make around here, and you're living quite literally hand to mouth, you never actually get one foot ahead of the other. You say to yourself, well, there is one thing I can do for myself. If there is some way I can make a few bucks and stay home at the same time, then hang up the factory job cause you're not going to get ahead anyway, so you may as well stay home and not get ahead. . . .

Further, respondents were often aware of these macrosocial differences, particularly for women:

> It's (a career) very attractive if you are well-educated, a professional woman who can go and take an office job where you start at $20,000, and the only way is up. You know, where within five years they own their own business. It sounds very good in "Cosmopolitan" magazine, but for the average housewife in a rural area in the state of Maine, that's ludicrous. Here it's what would you rather do, cook and wash, and look after the kids at home, or go into the shoeshop? You have the choice.

Other factors mentioned by the participants which encouraged home work were the high costs of transportation where distances are far and public transportation nonexistent, and the difficulty of getting around on winter roads.

Factors such as these, while rarely explicitly highlighted by the home workers themselves who usually offered more positive rationales for their employment choices, nonetheless form an undeniable backdrop. In examining how families allocate their time and space in the micro setting, the potential influence of the macro setting should not be neglected. Such attention to the macrosystem—that is, the broader social context—does not negate or vitiate the transferability of results, however. To the contrary, it offers a more profound appreciation of the strategies families employ to interact with that context. More importantly, potential similar studies comparing families from distinctive contexts (home workers in Detroit, Navajo craft families, executive consultants, etc.) allow the researcher to sort out the truly relevant influences from the less crucial ones and ultimately strengthen common findings.

The following pages carefully report the results obtained by looking at home-working families in this light. Rather than philosophizing or rhapsodizing about integration, the results adhere closely to the actual homely details of their daily lives. The disparate fragments currently constituting the definition of integration have been gathered primarily from the overly abstract ideal and the concretely negative impediments. Glaringly, the absent piece is the actual experience of families who are positively and pragmatically attempting to integrate work and family lives. For this reason, care is taken in the following pages to root the discussion of integration firmly in their very real daily lives and to appreciate the diversity of concrete ways in which they try to live out an ideal.

Chapter 4

Time and Space in Home-working Families*

The separate workplace also represented for men a
possible retreat from intimacy, as it may continue to
do today for some people. (Kanter 1977, 14)

Women have that tradition—they've been brought up
having a thousand and one little jobs to do around the
house every day. And sometimes you can't fulfill them
all, or you can't even fulfill one individual one, but
you have to attack each problem as it comes up. There
is breakfast, there is dinner, there is lunch or whatever, and each of them has to be taken care of. The
man is used to leaving the home, going to work,
punching the card—he does four hours right there at
a very specific time—then he has his lunch and he
punches that card again and works another four
hours. It's great because the woman has a completely
different attitude. The time is very fluid for a woman.
It's like the tide going in and out. Whereas for a man
it's like a drawbridge coming down and going up.
(Househusband of a home worker)

L essons from history implicate background factors of time
and space as influential yet subtle melders of work and

---

*Portions of the information reported in this chapter appeared in:
Beach, B. "Time Use in Rural Home-working Families" *Family Relations, 36,* (October 1987) pp 412–416.

family interaction. As we have seen, work space siting markedly affected the diverging development of men's and women's work and family expectations, with pervasive and enduring consequences. The departure of work from the home accomplished far more than a simple physical removal, leading as it did to major realignments in gender role expectations, in children's connections with work, and in men's and women's experiences of work. Space as a concept completely revolutionized previous historical encounters between work and family, marking for men an end to integration and initiating for women an ambivalent struggle to maintain it. So thoroughly and profoundly did workspace separation succeed that it banished the idea of diversity in work siting from our vocabulary. Now, our unquestioned assumption is that work occurs in physically distant settings generally inaccessible to family members and it is only the unusual study that considers space as a variable affecting family-work interaction.

Time, in contrast, presents a somewhat more familiar face to working families although historical precedents for considering it are infrequently applied. As work left the home setting in the nineteenth century, experiences of work time also followed disparate gender paths. Men, employed away from home, conformed to standardized, time-measured work days while women, working at home, retained the premodern task orientation attuned to natural rhythms rather than mechanical regulation. Such distinctions fashion a portrayal of women's work experiences as different from men's—different but not inherently inferior. Subtly, men's experiences of the segregated work space and regulated work time became the standard expectation for so-called real work, a measure against which women's more diverse work experiences were inevitably found wanting.

Despite history's signalling of the importance of space and time in investigating work-family issues, social science's response to the signal has been weak. Only systems theorists, seeking to connect families to broader social systems, have explicitly heeded the call by acknowledging time and space as crucial factors in family analysis, albeit not with the degree of longitudinality applied by historians. Generally, contemporary researchers disregard space as a variable, assuming implicitly

that workspace will be discrete, distant, inaccessible, and unfamiliar to family members. They do employ time as a variable, but not with the complexity history suggests it merits.
Recognized as a stressor for working families, time is most
commonly conceptualized as a concrete resource to be allocated; typically, studies look at how working families parcel
out time (hours and minutes) to work, child care, and household labor. They do not generally consider how individual experiences or perceptions of time might differ, nor that there
might be any gender-related distinctions. Standards of segregated work places and regulated work days prevail in most
such literature, a mark of how thoroughly the male model of
work has prevailed.

For home-working families, however, the assumption of
such standards of space and time must be questioned. Clearly
space, the chief distinguishing characteristic of home-
working families, promises quite a different context for relating work and family. Examining how home-working families
utilize space, then, is an important first step in studying
their lives. Knowing that history underscores its power to affect work and family roles, the researcher was cautious to
consider it carefully as a variable and indeed, space proved to
be a potent category of analysis. Correspondingly, history
hints that time may merit more attention to its complexity,
suggesting that it may be far more than a simple bundle of
minutes to be allocated. Exploring how home-working families utilize time and space creates an initial context for understanding other facets of their lives, at least if historical
lessons are to be credited. Finally, and not ironically, families'
use of time and space speaks to the heart of the issue of integration. As unarticulated as an integrated work-family relationship may be, an intuitive centrality is the wish to be more
available and accessible to family members, to spend more
time with them and/or to see children other than before and
after day care. Greater fluidity between work and family
boundaries is the underlying theme, a fluidity which examination of time and space use can make tangible. It is also
hard to escape the parallel with women's lives in such an investigation. Home work has historically been women's work;
do contemporary home workers retain some of the linkages

with premodern time and integrated space use that historical lessons suggest? Are home-working men's experiences of time and space use different from women's? Do home workers have a distinctive repetoire of space and time use, and if so, does it speak to the issue of integration?

THE USE OF SPACE

Despite a general lack of appreciation for space as a significant variable in work-family interaction, a few social scientists have suggested some helpful rudimentary approaches. Bolstering the argument of feminists who advocate home work as a means to diminish gender-role rigidities are writers suggesting that joining work and family space may indeed lessen stereotyping. Becker (1981) suggests that, minimally, transferring work to home may cause confusion in roles since traditionally "the physical separation of settings had provided a convenient cue for switching roles" (p. 187). Kanter (1977) expressed a similar sentiment, positing that the physical withdrawal of work from the home may also have afforded men a "retreat from intimacy"—a dramatic lessening of their former involvement in domestic life. Viewpoints such as these, encouraging the consideration of space as a significant influence in the work-family dynamic, nonetheless are primarily based in theory and/or interpretation. Although helpfully pointing the way, the exact dynamic by which space might affect family functioning remains uninvestigated.

For the work-at-home family, space indeed proved a potent analytical tool, a simple physical factor which dramatically shaped the family's relationship to work. Initially and concretely, shared space placed the work system in the family's midst (though the decision to share work and family space originated in individual actions, so perhaps the locus of influence belongs there). A workspace no longer impenetrable to family interaction permits family members to be present during work, to become involved in work, and to affect the course of the workday. Space as an analytical tool pervades the relationship of family and work, both on a profound level—what insights can a husband develop about his spouse as he watches her work? What is the nature of sex roles in such families?—and a simple level—what kinds of rules exist to restrict children's access? Are their playthings left lying around the workspace? I coded interviews for references to space use, and observations for actual use by family members. I combined information from these sources to generate a concept of how space is utilized in home-working families and how this particular use might affect work-family interaction.

The simplest initial categorization of work space was based on precise location: whether work space was located within the home space (for example, living room or kitchen), or in a separate area devoted exclusively to work (a shop or office in the ell). Working at home encompasses a range of options for precise physical siting, and the choice of that siting might indicate some important features of work and family spatial integration. Given both historical messages and contemporary suggestions about home work, the most obvious initial category of analysis for the use of space was sex. Do women and men differ in their use of space for working and living? Broken down by sex of worker, the following workspace usage emerged:

Table 4–1
Workspace Use by Sex of Worker (n=15)

Sex	Homespace	Category of Workspace Combined Home & Separate Space	Separate Space
Males	0	2	4
Females	7	1	1

Women, it appears from this breakdown, are more likely than men to utilize workspace within the home (seven women, no men); only one woman (a hairdresser) employed a separate shop devoted exclusively to her work. Women reported working at their dining room or kitchen tables and in the living room. Subsequent observations confirmed these reports, although with added flexibility:

H: There is no actual separate work area—the living room space, the table that Janet works on to sew the sweaters, is the table we use to eat from. . . . The chair that Janet sits in to sew the sweaters by hand is the chair she would sit in to watch television anyway. There is only one very small corner which might be segregated where the actual boxes of sweaters are kept, and that's about it. The work space can be anywhere actually. When Janet didn't feel well, she actually did some laying on the bed. That kind of thing.

W: My back ached last week. John brought them upstairs and I spent all the time . . . (working in bed).

Observations indicated that women working within the home space frequently shared that space with a preschool child. Six of the seven women working within the home space had young children (or grandchildren) present during observations. Thus, the presence of young children either necessitated the use of home space in order to supervise child care, or the use of home space allowed children to be present. Since women most commonly cited the presence of young children as the rationale for working at home, it seems more likely that they preferred home space in order to integrate children into their presence. The following excerpt from an observation illustrates how home work space and child care may be shared:

8:30: Arrival—greeted by M. J. (a seamstress) and four-year-old daughter Darcy. At the dining room table, M. lays out fabric, pins on pieces. She settles D. at table as well, who colors. As she cuts, she discusses buying a new car. D. asks for more paper, M. says, "We have some," goes for paper, "Look at all these pieces here," puts D. back to work. Returns to cutting pattern . . . As table shakes, she notes husband is building a new table "so I won't break my back." Replaces pieces (home made pattern) in pattern bag. D. is still drawing, says "Cap fell." M: "You can get it yourself." Dog approaches and she talks to him. Discusses children while cutting.

8:50: Checks off on master list as each pattern is done. "Guess I need more green" (fabric). As she leaves table pauses to look at D.'s picture and say, "That's nice!" Fetches fabric, returns to table, talks to daughter while cutting about daughter's impending heart surgery: "Tell B. about the hospital," "What's the name of that special test?" etc. D. still drawing. M. cutting teddy bear pattern, talking about children. Alternately stands and sits. D. jiggles table repeatedly, but no complaint from mother. D. "I want more paper."

M: "There's more there. Do you want me to tear it off?" (Stops to do so). "I guess we need more soon." Returns to cutting.

I also examined work space use through public contact, in the expectation that persons in occupations requiring a high and continuous degree of public contact in their work would need more isolated, non-home workspace. Men dominated in the category of public contact jobs (four out of six jobs), the only female positions being the previously mentioned hairdresser and a woman serving as secretary for a family business (see Table 4–2).

Table 4–2
Public Contact Job Workspace Use by Sex (n=l5)

Sex	Homespace	Category of Workspace Combined Home & Separate Space	Separate Space
Males	0	1	3
Females	0	1	1

By this measure as well, then, men were less likely to integrate their work space directly into their living space due to the nature of their jobs. Presumably, the high degree of public contact associated with men's jobs prohibited locating within family space. Such a factor merely reinforces the previous finding that women are more disposed to integrate work and family space than men but only partially explains why. Is it something mysterious about being female that inclines women toward greater shared space? Is it that women are naturally less likely to be in public contact jobs?

The most powerful explanatory factor for male-female space use came, unsurprisingly, from children. The linkage of women and young children most clearly paralleled integration of space. Distinguishing families with preschool children (up to six years of age) from families with only school-aged children (all children over seven years) produced the distribution shown in Table 4–3.

Distilling relationships between work and family based on location of workspace suggests the following characteristics:

Table 4–3
Workspace Use by Sex of Worker and Age of Children (n=15)

Group	Homespace	Category of Workspace Combined Home & Separate Space	Separate Space
Parents of Preschoolers			
Men	0	0	2
Women	6	0	1
Parents of Schoolaged Children Only			
Men	0	2	2
Women	1	1	0

1. That women are more likely to integrate home and workspace than men.

2. That men are more likely to be in public contact jobs necessitating separate work space than women.

3. That the presence of children under six years is the most powerful correlate of joint home/workspace.

4. That mothers of young children are more likely to work at home than fathers of young children.

While workspace location within the home suggests certain patterns, the degree of family accessibility to that workspace extends our understanding of how the two interact. Thus, a second category of analysis is, to use Piotrkowski's (1978) phrase, permeability of workspace—are families allowed free access to workspace, or are there restrictions on access? What are the consequences of such access?

Importantly, all workers reported that their spouse and children had free access to their work, a report generally corroborated by children in their interviews. Further, observations disclosed children present and interacting with working parents for all but three of the participants (their children were in school during observation periods). Even parents in public contact jobs permitted children's access to them; three of the public contact parents involved their children overtly in their work, two allowed their preschool children ready access, and only one placed slight restrictions on her children. Her comment:

W: They both (6F, 9F) enjoy lots of days like school vacations when they are home and everyone clears out of the office except me. (At such times, children can come and play in the office). They'll come out and they'll work at the back table and they've used stencils or things—they use the colored pencils and—

C (6F): That's the part daddy doesn't like!

H: They are getting so they are pretty good at it—I would say it gives them a good role model. They draw survey maps and they draw soil tests and they do a pretty good job.

Under questioning, parents in public contact jobs acknowledged that their children knew implicit rules of behavior, however. Because the children had shared the workspace for so long, they had absorbed behavioral expectations about dealing with the public that other children did not possess. For example, as one father (a chef) described it:

H: Well, say I'm working in the kitchen here and you're three years old and you're sitting across the counter basically in the way, or you're down here watching and just kind of being around, and a noise is made or something happens. My immediate reaction is, shhh, there are people in the restaurant. If that starts when the child is three, he grows up with the fact that, (whispers) "there are people eating out there, you'd better be quiet." I think they just grew up with that sort of attitude. I don't think it was ever verbalized.

Despite this slight difference in consciousness among children of public contact occupations, the point about space most deserving of emphasis is its ready permeability to family members. For work-at-home families, then, space is a crucial medium facilitating the interaction rather than the isolation of work and family systems. Contrasted with the impervious boundaries of most conventional workplaces which are aimed at repelling family interaction, shared home and workspace invites casual interplay of spouse, children, and worker. Even individuals in public contact jobs permit ready access. Such a merging of home and workspace sets the stage for several potentially distinctive work and family behaviors. For most American children, their parents' workplace is a foreign culture, distant, inaccessible, and unfamiliar, "not one that children enter often or for very long periods of time. Its status is . . . that of an exosystem" (Bronfenbrenner 1979, 236). What happens to children's perceptions of their parents and work when that work is accessible and familiar? History suggests that a joint work and home space such as manifested by home-working families also involved different perceptions of time, with greater flow between work and family responsibilities rather than rigid allocations. Does the permeability of space indicated by these families carry over into a permeability of time? Some feminist writers (Boneparth and Stoper 1983) advocate greater work-at-home opportunities because they believe that shared space inevitably promotes a breakdown in rigid gender-role expectations. Does this happen in home-working families? Do joint home and work spaces encourage engagement rather than retreat?

Shared home and work space offers an initial measure of integration. Shared space is an enabler, a first step toward a fuller model of integration. Families' own next steps enlarge that initial definition.

THE USE OF TIME

Time is a precious commodity to working parents. Time pressures emerge repeatedly as stressors in fulfilling work and family responsibilities, whether in large scale surveys, or in smaller interview studies. Consequently, many studies, recognizing time as a key ingredient in work-family relations, have focused on some aspect of time use: general studies of time allocation to work and household duties, effects of work schedules on families, or impacts of work schedule innovation on family life. Such studies have their popular counterparts in magazine articles detailing harried women workers, overloaded parents and the burn-out syndrome, their common core being insufficient time to fulfill a myriad of responsibilities on the home and work fronts. Implicit in most such articles is the use of time as a finite tool of analysis, readily quantifiable, a scarce resource to be allocated. For contemporary workers who are held to an exacting standard first developed when men entered the industrial world, this represents an adequate conceptualization of time. Indeed, most Americans labor under the segregated concept of time: regulated by the clock, inflexibly allocated, rigidly compartmentalized from non-work time needs. For them, time is clearly a scarce resource to be allocated.

But what about alternative conceptions of time? Again, we have the historical suggestion of divergence between men's and women's experiences, with men adapting of necessity to the new regulated structure of industrial time while women, remaining in the home, retained the natural rhythms and responsiveness of preindustrial time. One of home work's presumed advantages for nineteenth-century women was its flexibility and responsiveness to other, more pressing household needs. Did such a different conception of time really exist? If so, does it have any present-day counterparts, or are we all socialized uniformly to time as dictated by the mechanical timepiece?

Most time use studies subscribe to the latter concept and, quite rightly, note the obstacles to integrating which it erects. Staying home with a sick child, attending a school event, or taking time for a family need all subtract from work time, and represent a collision between the segregated model's definition of work as dictated by the clock and what a more integrated model might favor. Not coincidentally, such envisioning of time as a resource to be allocated supports the prevailing work model based on men's experiences. However, other more small scale and qualitative researchers caution that time may not be as readily amenable to quantification as published results indicate, and that time use may be more complex than survey results superficially indicate, particularly for women:

> We would urge more use of time studies with working families. Our own efforts in this study convinced us of the difficulties in obtaining valid and reliable time-use data. Time is used in multiple ways simultaneously, and there are consequent problems in allocating time segments to discrete tasks. "The laundry is put into the machine and while the wash is done I get dinner ready. The four-year-old likes to help so she puts the plates and silver on the table. The baby is in the high chair and we sing songs and play together.

Sometimes I give the baby supper then." How are we to allocate this half-hour? Yet despite the difficulty we need to know more about how working parents use their time. (Kamerman 1980, 134)

Reports on time use data from home workers support the latter concern: that time is not as readily quantifiable or apportionable as large scale surveys indicate. Data on time use (interviews, observations, and time logs) in this study underscored not the importance of *allocation* of time but instead its *flexibility*. While most studies conceive of time as a resource to be allocated among competing demands, families here valued it as a responsive medium. Rather than representing a finite resource to be distributed in segments (for example, eight hours to work, two hours to commuting, one hour to quality child interaction), time for work-at-home families was less uniform, more flexible, and more integrated with daily functions. Participants reported variable work days of non-uniform hours, punctuated by breaks for specific needs—a child's violin lessons, decorating a birthday cake, doing laundry or reading to a child. Although not unmindful of the need to perform certain quantities of work (which they seemed to do in a disciplined manner), home workers more closely resembled the premodern use of time described by Thompson (1967) rather than the discipline imposed by industrialization. The following summary of time use cites data from daily logs and observations in order to examine the content and division of the workday for home workers. As their days interweave work and family activities, they begin to create a sense of what integration might involve on the simplest of levels.

LOGS

I asked each home worker to submit logs listing daily activities for two days. They returned a total of twenty-six daily logs, of which twenty-two were analyzable. Six sample logs are included here for the purpose of indicating their complexity, ranging from the fairly simple to the more complicated (Logs 4–1, 4–2, 4–3, 4–4, 4–5, 4–6).

Sample Log 4–1
DAILY LOG

Date: 4/26/84

Work Activities	*Non-Work Activities*
Start work time: 8:00	*Activity*: Kindergarten
Finish work time: 3:00	Registration
Special comments on work	Time Started: 3:00
schedule:	Stopped: 4:15
1/2 hr. for lunch	*Activity*: Clean up shop
	Time Started: 4:15
	Stopped: 4:30

Sample Log 4–2
DAILY LOG

Date: 4/6/84

Work Activities	*Non-Work Activities*
Start work time: 8:00	*Activity*: Dishes, Laundry,
Finish work time: 4:30	Feed cat, Puzzle
Special comments on	with daughter.
work schedule:	Time Started: 9:30
Tax Map copies	Stopped: 10:15
Typing	*Activity*: Prepare lunch,
Bookkeeping—Closed books	dishes
for Fiscal Year	Time Started: 11:30
Banking—Business	Stopped: 12:10
Inking	*Activity*: Fold laundry, fill
Quarterly Tax Deposit Forms	wood box, Walk to
Filing	stream, violin with
	daughter
	Time Started: 3:00
	Stopped: 3:30

Sample Log 4–3
DAILY LOG

Date: 4/9/84

Work Activities	*Non-Work Activities*
Start work time: 8:00	*Activity*: Laundry

Finish work time: 6:00
*Special comments on
    work schedule.*
Monday is a long day this
week. My daughter's birthday
is tomorrow, so I had to do
as much as possible.

Time Started: 9:15
    Stopped: 9:35
Activity: Lunch
Time Started: 11:30
    Stopped: 12:30
Activity: Kids came home
Time Started: 2:45
    Stopped: 3:10
Activity: Started Supper
Time Started: 4:30
    Stopped: 5:00

Sample Log 4–4
DAILY LOG

Date: 6/5/84
Work Activities
Start work time: 9:00
Finish work time: 9:40
    made calls
read trade paper, etc.
*Special comments on
    work schedule*:
11:10–12:15 customer
3:30–3:45 customer
7:00–7:40 picked out
    frame & packed samples
    to be returned
As you can see, work occurs
when it happens or when it
can be squeezed in.

Non-Work Activities
Activity: Dressed, fed kids
    breakfast
Time Started: 7:00
    Stopped: 8:30
Activity: Went downtown for
    paper and mail with
    children
Time Started: 8:30
    Stopped: 9:00
Activity: outdoor work with
    children
Time Started: 10:30
    Stopped 11:10
Activity: Errands—New tire
    dump
Time Started: 12:15
    Stopped: 3:30
Activity: Sat around talked
    with wife, sitter
Time Started: 3:45
    Stopped: 4:15
Activity: Cooked dinner and
    ate, and washed
    dishes

Time Started: 4:15
   Stopped: 6:00
Activity: read two books and
            put kids to bed
Time Started: 6:00
   Stopped: 6:30
Activity: Watched news
Time Started: 6:30
   Stopped: 7:00
Activity: Went out for ice
            cream
Time Started: 7:40
   Stopped: 8:10
Activity: Read, Watched TV
Time Started: 8:10
   Stopped: 10:00

Sample Log No. 4–5
DAILY LOG

Date: 4/14/84
Work Activities
Start work time: 8 AM
Finish work time: 10 PM
*Special comments on
   work schedule*:

Non-Work Activities
Activity: Start bread
Time Started: 8:30
   Stopped: 8:40
Activity: Changed record for
            Alice, got her an
            orange
Time Started: 9:10
   Stopped: 9:12
Activity: Mixed bread, got
            Alice dressed to go
            out
Time Started: 9:20
   Stopped: 9:35
Activity: Outhouse
Time Started: 9:55
   Stopped: 10:05
Activity: Family activities,
            lunch garden, start
            sauna

Time Started: 10:15
   Stopped: 1:20
Activity: see to bread, sauna
         fine
Time Started: 1:45
   Stopped: 1:55
Activity: Tea break, sauna
Time Started: 2:20
   Stopped: 3:30
Activity: Supper, got Alice to
         bed
Time Started: 4:30
   Stopped: 7:00
Activity:
Time Started: Stopped:

Sample Log No. 4–6
DAILY LOG

Date: 6/1/84

Work Activities
Start work time: 7:30AM
Finish work time: 4PM
*Special comments on
   work schedule*:
I generally work during the
evening starting around 7:30
ending anywhere from 10:00
to 11:00. I find that this time
is more of a "jumping-jack"
period than during the day.

Non-work Activities
Activity: Child care, break-
         fast, start wash
Time Started: 9:00
   Stopped: 9:30
Activity: read story, hung
         wash
Time Started: 10:05
   Stopped: 10:25
Activity: phone call re:
         child's med.
Time Started: 11:12
   Stopped: 11:25
Activity: Phone call out re:
         child's med.
Time Started: 11:40
   Stopped: 11:50
Activity: Lunch, errands,
         started fire
Time Started: 12:30
   Stopped: 2PM

> *Activity*: two phone calls out
> re: child's med.
> Time Started: 3:30
> Stopped: 3:45

Salient features of the logs fell into the following categories:

1. Lack of a standard work day: For these participants, there was no approximation of a prototypical work day. The concept of the straightforward, uninterrupted, compartmentalized workday proved irrelevant to this group. The group reported work days ranging from a low of two hours and fifty minutes to eleven hours and fifty minutes. (These figures are the reported parameters of the work day, that is, the start work and stop work times reported). This variability in work hours also applied to individuals within the group: no individual reported the same work schedule on the two days. Sample logs 4–1 and 4–2 most closely resemble the conventional work day in daily schedule reported; however, the second logs for each of these participants displayed greater variability in hours worked.

The earliest reported start work time was 6:00 A.M.; the latest reported stop work time was 11:00 P.M.. Starting and stopping times generally ranged within those figures, with most people finishing anywhere between 2:30 and the evening hours.

Length of day worked was more difficult to allocate. Subtracting reported non-work activities from work activities resulted in a range of actual hours worked from a low of 170 minutes (2.8 hours) to a high of 810 minutes (13.5 hours). The average reported work time was 404 minutes (6.73 hours) per person. Though this reported work time is less than the proverbial eight-hour workday, several cautions must be employed in interpreting such results: (1) These logs are based on precise individual reports which naturally vary with the individual's dutifulness (witness Sample log 4–5 which delineates a ten-minute visit to the outhouse). (2) Most data on workday length results from aggregate, estimated time rather than accurate individual timekeeping; such large scale surveys mask variability in individual interpretation and accuracy of work time data. (3) Several participants in this sample reported doing additional work in the evening, simultaneously watching TV, talking with children, visiting with friends, etc., but do not report this as work time. As an example, Sample Log 4–6 reports her work day as extending from 7:30 A.M. to 4:00 P.M., but adds the comment: "I generally work during the evening starting around 7:30 P.M. ending anywhere from 10:00 P.M. to 11:00 P.M. I find that this time is more of a 'jumping jack' period than during the days." (4) The imbalance of women to men in this study may slant the reported work time. Most studies indicate that women prefer to work part-time when they have families and indeed that part-time work may be optimal for such women. Results in this study may reflect women's ability to choose that schedule.

2. Work day punctuated by interruptions: All workers reported interruptions to their work day, whether for personal or family chores. Although it is not unusual for conventionally employed workers to take time off work to attend to such chores, the ease and frequency with which home workers did so was striking. Obviously, space was a critical factor in allowing such interruptions: shared work and family space permitted a flow in interaction not possible when work and family boundaries are physically distinct and clearly demarcated.

I further analyzed logs for number of interruptions to the reported work day, length of such interruptions, and nature of such interruptions. The latter classification fell readily into the following categories: household chores, child tends (discrete initiations or responses to children), leisure, errands. Table 4–4 summarizes the interruption data (listed as non-work activities by the participants).

Initial working conclusions reached from analysis of interruptions to workday show that women have shorter workdays which contained twice as many interruptions as men's workdays. These interruptions are both more frequent and of shorter duration than men's, creating a picture of an abbreviated back and forth interaction between work and family functions. Consistent with other research findings that men are more likely to increase their child care role rather than their housework role, there is little difference between men's and women's reported child care tends. The most glaring con-

Table 4–4
Mean Number, Duration and Nature of Interruptions to Workday
By Sex: Log Analysis

Sex of Worker	Number	Interruptions Duration (in minutes)	Nature
Men (n=4) 8 logs	4	45.5	2.1 Household
			.7 Child Tend
			.5 Errand
			.5 Leisure
Women (n=7) 14 logs	7	32	4.8 Household
			1.3 Child Tend
			.6 Leisure
			.1 Errand

trast is seen in household duties where women perform twice as many housework chores as men.

However satisfactory such quantitative findings appear, some cautions must be put forth. The most notable deficiency is the inability of the log method to capture the real work of women: the constant, ongoing interaction with children who are present while they work. One woman acknowledged this difficulty in comments on her log: "None of this (reported work day) includes 'dog and cat' duty as well as 'little calls for help' from Darcy." The difficulty of measuring ongoing simultaneous activities has been acknowledged by other researchers, particularly in the study of housework. Since women have traditionally worked simultaneously fulfilling parental, household and, in this case, paid work duties, it is the female experience that has been glossed over rather than the male.

To counter or confirm tentative findings from logs about workdays, I examined observations for insights. Observational notes were anecdotal, reporting everything occurring to the home worker during the two-hour observation period. They were not precoded and thus made no attempt to fit the observed activities into preconceived schemes or categories. Instead, observations were simply coded afterward for instances of household chores observed or children tended. I did not record precise time devoted to each chore, and thus reports on observations lack the attractive exactitude of minutes apportioned. Observations also occurred during the worker's self-described work time and thus might be expected to portray more work than non-work activities. These limitations aside, observations assisted in remedying some of the deficiencies noted in the log methodology and in amplifying some of its findings.

A critical feature of the observations was to penetrate the facade of work time reported by the participants. While all log reporters ascribed certain amounts of time to work activities in a straightforwardly measurable manner, observations of their designated work times revealed that this time was not nearly as monolithic or discrete as numerical reports might promise. Of thirty observations, only one displayed no interruptions to work activity during the two-hour period. Interruptions fell readily into six categories, the distribution of which is listed below (thirty observations/fifteen participants):

Tend to child: 127 occurrences

Household chore: 34 occurrences

Break/relax: 21 occurrences

Phone conversation (non-business): 8 occurrences

Shortened work time (for example, stop early to greet children arriving home from school): 6 occurrences

Spouse business (messages or phone call in support of spouse's work): 6 occurrences

Clearly, work time encompasses significant amounts of non-work activities which do not appear in log form. Most interruptions take place for child tending, excerpted examples of which appear below. Each is an example of one coded "tend."

Father, Todd, is working on business matters at desk in the gallery of his home:

10:35—Todd takes watercolor off wall, places it against door to outdoors, snaps a Polaroid. Nate (4M) is still working quietly on floor with Legos. . . . Baby sister starts grabbing Nate's Legos), Mother suggests that Nate use Pa's desk "unless you need it." Todd says he's working but Nate can have room. He clears off front of desk (Sheraton table). Nate runs out and returns with a Windsor high chair which he places at table to play. Todd starts typing at electric typewriter, sister runs over to corner to ride on rocking horse. Nate and Dad at table working (Legos and typing).

Seamstress mother is sewing at machine:

Darcy (4F) comes over to bench, picks up fabric hole punch, "Look at this beautiful color." Mo: "Yes" Darcy: "What color is it?" Mo: "You know it's silver." Darcy: "What do you use this for?" Mo: "I used it before I got the new one. It's for snaps." Darcy: "Can I use it?" Mo: "Just don't lose the little white plastic parts." Darcy sits at the dining room table with paper and punch. "I can use it." Counts punches. Chats over what she is doing, keeps counting each time she works punch.

A knitter working in her kitchen:

1:15: Stops to recheck procedure for curving yoke. "This is the part I hate" requiring decrease of stitches. Stands to adjust tension, rethreads yarn, resumes back and forth of carriage, binds off.

1:20: Noise from Karen's (2F) room where she is napping. Mo. gets up, goes into her room, talks with her, turns TV on for her. Returns to table, "OK, where was I?"

Such vignettes provide a flavor of how a work-at-home parent might interrupt his/her work time to tend to a child. Naturally, these interruptions (what one parent labelled "little calls for help") were unrecorded in logs because they occurred during work time. Table 4–5, based on the twenty observations during which children were present, indicates the distribution of interruptions for child tending.

Table 4–5
Mean Number of Child Tends per Two Hour Observation by Sex

Sex	No. of Child Tends
Men (n=6)	5.28
Women (n=9)	6.92

Such results indicate that women have slightly more child care interruptions during their work time than do men, echoing the log reports that women interrupt their total workday more frequently for child care. Such a table masks other important variables, however, including degree of spousal participation, age of children, and motivations for working at home. Reconceptualizing the "tend" category by age of children predictably portrays dramatic disparity between households where preschool-aged children were present during observations versus houses where only school-aged children were present as seen in Table 4–6.

Table 4–6
Mean Number of Child Tends per Two Hour Observation by Age of Child

Age of Child	No. of Child Tends
Preschoolers (0–6)	8.30
Schoolage (7–18)	2.71

Thus, age of children appears to be a major factor influencing the course of the workday. Since women are more likely to have younger children at home, children powerfully affect the course of women's workday—not an unsurprising finding to anyone who has ever spent a day in the company of preschoolers. The linkage of women, young children, co-existing work and family space, and interrupted workdays is strongly intertwined. Men appear to be slightly more aloof, buffered by being in separated home workspaces and having older children requiring less tending. Are men less capable of handling simultaneous work and family chores, or simply less disposed to do so? Regardless of this disparity, emphasis needs to be firmly placed on the fact that home-working men do indeed attend to children and household chores during the day. The family accessibility afforded by the home workspace facilitates a flow of interaction which no man tried to stem. All men were involved in the daily lives of their children and spouses; no one succeeded in isolating himself completely in an effort to replicate the work model of the world. Thus, while men tended to differ in quantity of interpenetration of time and space, the type of interaction they displayed was essentially the same as women's. In other words, time and space appear to be integrated for both sexes, though more so for women; however, working at home appears to encourage task sharing among these families for both men and women.

THE IMPORTANCE OF PHENOMENOLOGY

Thus far, we have seen that sex of parent and age of child rank as important variables in measuring interruptions to

Table 4–7

Observed Performance of Child Tends per Two Hour Observation by Sex of Parent and Work Motivation

Group	No. of Observations involving children (2 per participant)	No. of Tends Per 2 Obs.	Mean Tends Per Obs.
Family Motivations			
Men (2)	4	31	7.75
Women (8)	13	90	5.62
Non-Family Motivations			
Men (4)	3	6	1.5
Women (1)	0	0	0
15	20	127	

the workday. However, an even more important phenomenological factor lurks in the background: that of rationale for working at home. Eight out of nine women and two out of six men reported family motivations (spending more time with children, being available to family, etc.) as their prime rationale for working at home. These individuals account for the vast bulk of the child care tends observed, expecially when examining the entire total of thirty observations. Of the thirty observations completed, twenty had children present; of the ten where children were not present, seven were accounted for by individuals citing other than family rationales for working at home. In other words, people who wanted to spend more time with their families and deliberately chose home work to do so were indeed more inclined to have children present. This rationale even superseded sex as an explanatory factor, for when family vs. non-family motivations for working at home are considered, and the missing ten observations are added in to the total of child tends, a different picture is created (Table 4–7):

Of all the major variables, then, the greatest potential distinction is provided by phenomenology—men and women who cited family reasons for choosing to work at home are more similar to each other than to other members of their sex who chose other prime motivations for working at home such as self-employment or economics. Quite simply, those who wanted to integrate (male and female) demonstrated the highest degree of such integration vis-à-vis their children and interruptible workdays.

The less significant category of household chores disclosed similar results, thirty-four of which were observed to interrupt work activity. The specific breakdown of these chores follows:

Total number of chores observed in thirty observations: 34
Breakdown of total chores

Food preparation	11
Stoke fires	7
Laundry	3
Pet care	3
Yardwork	1
Dishes	1
Plant seeds	1
Wash car	1
Sort mail	1
Misc.	3

Although the overall average of household chores performed by men and women appears fairly similar (men = average of 2 chores performed, women = 2.44), a breakdown by family motivation is again instructive as seen in Table 4–8.

The other categories of work time interruptions were too scanty to merit analysis. Interestingly, these other categories (break/relax, personal phone calls, spouse business phone, and shortened work time) could also apply to conventionally

Table 4–8

Observed Performance of Household Chores per Two Hour Observation by Sex of Worker and Motivation (n=15)

Group	No. of Household Chores Observed in 2 observations	Mean per person per observation
Family Motivation		
Men (2)	6	1.5
Women (8)	21	1.3
Non-Family Motivation		
Men (4)	6	.7
Women (1)	1	.5

employed workers. Major interruptions of child care and household chores are less accessible to the latter group though they account for large segments of the home worker's time.

Summarizing briefly the information derived by the use of time and space as analytical tools, these families do not segregate work life and family life. All workers' families had space and time access to the work world. Refinement of quantitative data suggests that women are more likely to integrate the two more thoroughly than men: more likely to use domestic space as a worksite, to have children (especially preschool) present while working, to have a shorter, more frequently interrupted workday and work time, and to perform more household chores. However, results also suggest that, for some men, family motivation in choosing to work at home may make their work style more similar to women's. Men sharing a desire to integrate work and family life more evenly (a gender expectation usually accorded women) may construct a daily work life quite similar to women's. This hint that personal choice may forcefully affect the nature of the work structure should not be disregarded although the very small group size merely raises the possibility. Also not to be forgotten is the fact that all such workers held previous outside employment and made conscious, deliberate elections in choosing to work at home; consequently, one might infer that their present work patterns represent a personal preference of some sort, differentiating them in some way from most workers who fit into structures provided by conventional employment.

Despite these differences between women's and men's work space and time, and the suggestion of phenomenology as a potentially distinguishing feature of the home work experience, the pervasive ability of joint home and workspace to affect all workers' lives should not be overlooked. Regardless of motivation or particular job, all men and women were involved with their families' daily lives, permitting accessibility and living out an interspersing of work and family time and space. The degree of this interspersion varied, but the fact of its existence did not. For these families overall, the question of whether home work encourages greater integration of work and family life receives a resounding answer yes, certainly in space and time. Initially, home work sets the stage for fusing working and loving and the reports and observations of these families demonstrate graphically that this interplay exists. What next needs answering is the nature of this interplay for family life, the topics of the next chapters.

Chapter 5

The Homeworker: Blending Roles as Individual, Spouse, Parent

Well, I feel that your life should come first, you
know, your work should come second . . . it's
so easy for it (work) to become your entire life.
(A home-working father)

Enmeshed in the core of the work-family intersection is the
homeworker himself or herself, the individual who elects
the strategy and then lives out its consequences on a daily
basis. What does working at home signify for the individual
concerned? How does his/her day differ from the "outside"
work world? What are the mundane details of that life? Does
home work indeed translate into a form of integrating work
and family life? Are home workers and their families different
from other workers? Is home work an exploitive form of wom-
en's work, as some critics allege? Taking the time to sift patiently through the daily lives of home-working families is a
necessary first step in building understanding. Although un-
glamorous, attending to the real lives of real people in very
concrete ways must precede any wholehearted advocacy or
condemnation of home work as a strategy for integrating.
Working families' struggles to reconcile competing demands
usually emerge from small, pragmatic details: do I stay home
with my sick child and miss work, or do I send her to day

91

care? Do I attend this important meeting after working hours or do I watch my child play baseball? Do I say no to my boss or to my family? It is from examining these seemingly trivial experiences that a more profound sense of integration can emerge. The following results focus on the individual who has chosen home work as an alternative work strategy.

Two compelling characteristics emerged among home workers from interviews, observations and daily logs. One clustered around the worker himself/herself, creating an image of an individual who prizes work autonomy. The ability to control work process and schedule, to contrast it (unfavorably) with previous work experiences in conventional settings, and to recast work demands to fit family needs contributed to a portrayal of the autonomous worker, valuing his/her ability to be in charge. Equally true of women as men, this sense of autonomy underlay much of home work's appeal and success, even in view of comparative objective disadvantages such as the lack of employment benefits. Rather than speaking meekly, home workers' powerful voicing of the value of work independence suggests that they may appreciate more highly than most the benefits of autonomy, perceiving it as a desirable alternative to a work world esteeming conformity, submissiveness, and routine.

Complementing and interacting with a sense of autonomy was a second key characteristic: a reported feeling of family responsivity. Home workers felt they could (and did) orchestrate work demands to accommodate family needs. Very clearly, a family context underlay the home workers' role as family members became involved in home work, as work schedules were interrupted and recreated to meet family needs, and as work-family roles blurred. This partnership of autonomy and family responsivity begins to offer substance and definition to integration, and the circumstances which might encourage it. The pragmatic details of their daily lives offer some tangibility and a standard of comparison for assessing that integration.

THE AUTONOMOUS HOME WORKER

Autonomy on the job has been recognized by researchers as a potential variable in work-family interaction, Kanter even suggesting that "work autonomy or a similar emotional climate variable, such as control over work opportunities, may be more important than the gross measure of class. . . ." (Kanter 1977, 49). However, most of the limited research relating to job autonomy and families has been unidirectional, looking principally at how job conditions affect family life. Perhaps most familiar is investigation into employment and consequent child-rearing style, where researchers, looking at effects of paternal employment, have found self-direction and initiative-taking on the job to be associated with less restrictive child-rearing methods. Most researchers write implicitly from the vantage that middle class jobs allow more autonomy than blue collar jobs, without examining the specific context of those occupations; for these researchers, autonomy becomes a class-related code with little precise defining of what constitutes autonomy on the job. Partial answers have been offered by some researchers investigating work-family stress and job autonomy. Staines and Pleck (1983) concluded that some degree of schedule control is a significant moderating variable in reducing work-family stress. More qualitatively, Renshaw's (1976) study emphasized the value of "perceived influence"—the individual's perception of his/her control over the handling of work-family stress as a critical feature. There has been little movement beyond these suggestions to pin down the linkages between autonomy on the job and family effects and, more significantly, almost nothing looking at family effects on job autonomy.

In contrast to this background, the voices of home workers spoke loudly and convincingly. Although the question, "Are you autonomous on the job?" was never put to them, nor was it initially considered as a significant variable, their general responses to other questions provided a compelling theme interrelating autonomy, work, and family life. Their answers to questions about motivations for choosing home work, comparisons with other jobs, and satisfactions with work, as well as observations and log reports of time allocation, combined to create a body of data to analyze for conceptions of autonomy and its influence on work and family lives. Briefly, perceptions of autonomy fell into several major categories.

1. *Control over work process and time.* All participants expressed a sense of control over their work process and schedule. For some, this sense of autonomy was practical:

> W: It's   almost—you   might   as   well   say—complete
> freedom. . . . I mean if I was in the shoeshop or a mill doing
> this (working), I wouldn't be able to sit here and talk with
> you. When I want a cup of coffee, I can have a cup of coffee.
> I can sit there and I can have a cigarette. Most of my ciga-
> rettes burn up in the ash tray when I'm sitting working, but
> I can do whatever I want. And if right in the middle of a
> sweater I feel like up and going to town to buy something, I
> can get up and go.

And:

> I like to bake bread and it's nice to be able to sew a few
> sweaters and get up and mix the bread a little and sew a few
> more and get up and put it to rise and sew a few more. That
> type of thing is very convenient.

And:

> It is a wonderful sense of having the time completely at your
> disposal. And the advantage of being home is that when you
> feel like you need a break, very often there is something that
> needs to be done—like I take water down to the animals or
> something like that. So there is a kind of back and forth
> that can take place. . . .

And:

> If it's a real nice hot summer day, you know, there is no rea-
> son not to go to Reid State Park or Ogunquit for the day or
> whatever any time we want. That's the great part about the
> job. At any time you want to go anywhere you can go. . . . I
> feel that your life should come first and you know, your work
> should come second. . . .

Both observations and logs verified this sense of control over work and family life. Daily logs submitted by participants showed no workdays uninterrupted by personal or family ac-tivities. Of the thirty observations of work periods (two hour blocks x two per family), time spent directly on work-related activity ranged from a low of ten minutes to a more conven-tional, nearly two hours, evidencing considerable variability

and control over work time. However, amount of time alone
was not as indicative of autonomy as much as interruptibility
was. Particularly for women working at home, work time was
frequently interrupted and observations were made of women
putting work aside to read to a preschooler, greet a child returning from school, answer questions, look over school
work, take a child to violin lessons or care for a sick child.
Men tended to be more consistent in their work time (obviously partly due to the absence of young children) but only
one man was self-described and subsequently observed working a nearly prototypical eight-hour workday. Home workers
instead characterized their workdays as never typical, variable
by day, hours, and season. While all reported working an estimated number of hours per week, variations in work schedules were more commonly reported and observed than
conventional work schedules. For individual workers, any two
days of logs reflected this variation.

2. *Negatives of outside work experience phrased in lack
of autonomy.* Control over time and process, then, was a salient feature of occupational autonomy for these participants,
revealed in self-descriptions and verified by observations and
time logs. Autonomy had another crucial component cited by
eleven out of fifteen participants—freedom from negative aspects of previous work experience, frequently couched in
terms of lack of autonomy.

> H: I can't stand to have somebody stand over my back and
> give me orders all the time. You know, a boss expects you to
> do it his way and you have your own way of doing it that will
> come out exactly the same. But, no, you've got to do it his
> way. And I can't hack that.

And:

> W: Oh, well, can I count the ways? The shoeshop closed. I
> worked there twice. . . . I quit about halfway through my
> pregnancy. But the atmosphere was terrible. The people who
> were in charge were little short of—I can't think of a polite
> enough word to describe them but, it wasn't a good atmo-
> sphere. I've worked in a few mills where, you know, there
> were nice people to work for and all the rest. It was as pleas-
> ant a job as I could get, but it's certainly not pleasant
> punching a time clock. I've never worked in a clean mill. I've

worked in plastics where you get the fumes. I actually would break out in hives. I was allergic to the materials in the plastic. In the woolen mills, there is dust, in the wood mills there is dust. In the shoeshop I refused to work on a couple of machines that I felt the fumes would harm me when I was pregnant. That is why I refused. They accepted it grudgingly.

And:

W: And the time deadlines too—there is no late for work or trying to get away early in the traffic. Also, I don't have to get all dressed up every day, which is something that I don't like to do.

And:

W: The pay is less (than the previous job) but I didn't like the pressure in the shop. In the mills you've got to go just as fast as you can to make enough money to stay there, especially on piece work. If you're on hour work, I don't know, I never worked hour work . . . cause with this here job (knitting), the more you do, the more money you're going to make. But you can set your own pace and you haven't got to go like blazes in order to keep the next guy from getting it all—the good work. . . . You don't have to fight for your work in other words.

And:

W: I liked my job (previously shoe worker), it wasn't a machine job, it was counting and your mind was working and it wasn't all that difficult, but you had to get certain things in the right piles and sizes in the right order. But it was the atmosphere, I just couldn't stand it. . . . This (present home knitting) would be the same thing if it were in a factory.

I: O.K. The knitting, as much as you like it, if you had to go out to a shop to do it, then you might not.

W: I wouldn't do it.

3. *Control over work schedule which allowed responsiveness to family needs.* A third critical feature emerged from the data: ability to respond to family needs. Mainstream writing on the topic of autonomy revolves around intraoccupational characteristics such as self-direction on job or placement in workplace hierarchy, ignoring the potential links

between job autonomy and family life. For these participants, however, a principal advantage of home work is the opportunity it affords to set aside, reschedule, increase or decrease work in order to accommodate particular family needs. Examples of this form of autonomy were cited in interviews and repeatedly displayed later in observations:

> W: I can make my own hours. You know, if he (baby) has a doctor's appointment or something and I just take the day off. . . . Or if I want to take the day off and go shopping or if my husband says, well, I'm going to take next Friday off, you know, like we took last Friday off and went skiing.

And:

> W: And that's the thing that's a real advantage as opposed to one or the other of us being obligated to working for someone else. He would have a day off and it would be a glorious day and we could go to the coast, but gee, Mom has to leave (for work) at 2:00 today, you know. That to me was more painful than any 11 o'clock nights or 7 o'clock mornings.

This sense of autonomy to respond to family needs, initially developed modestly in interviews, was amply and resoundingly verified in subsequent observations. Observations proved crucial in revealing newly arisen conditions, unexpected crises, or mundane concrete instances to which the worker was able to respond by manipulating job conditions: unexpected open heart surgery for a preschooler, the addition of a part-time job as a supermarket cashier, a child home sick from school, the need to take a three-week time intensive course, the opening of fishing season, Suzuki violin lessons with a child, volunteering in a local school program, and increasing involvement in an anti-nuclear group. All of these examples, and others, provide graphic support for the importance of the link between job autonomy and family life. Incidents such as those cited would present insurmountable barriers to people in conventional employment, intensifying the stress between work and family demands. By contrast, participants in this study responded by rearranging work conditions to meet these needs through rescheduling and increasing/decreasing workloads at necessary times. This responsiveness was universal—even workers involved in a larger organization (for example, knitters) retained this ability, either by increasing or grouping workloads at certain times, decreasing or refusing work, or calling upon family members for assistance.

   4. *Non-gregariousness.* For home workers, then, just as for conventionally employed people, autonomy can be a salient feature of their job. Autonomy here received concrete expression in a sense of control over time and work processes, negative perceptions of conventional employment relative to autonomy, and a positive ability to respond to family needs. This sense of autonomy as an individual was complemented by what I originally coded the "loner" factor, subsequently refined into a "non-gregarious" code after Robinson's (1977) description. Enjoying working on one's own contradicts commonly held assumptions about the workplace as a requisite source of socialization for adults; indeed much work literature is predicated on the assumption that the opportunity to socialize at work is a critical component of work experience. Sharply contrasting with this presumption are the statements of home workers who, though by no means isolate, hold disparate views about the necessity of workplace socialization. Their expressions of non-gregariousness provide an important reminder that not all workers conform to these expectations and that the sensible work organization might consider adapting itself to the needs of such workers. What I initially coded as the loner factor received direct expression by twelve of the fifteen home workers:

   W: I've always liked to be by myself and I really feel sorry for people who can't—you know, be alone and enjoy it.

And:

   H: No, ah, I'm not interested (in socializing). I mean, I'm really not interested in other people. . . .

And:

   H: I am a bit of a recluse.

And:

   And in some ways I have my own little philosophies about people being able to be independent of others and comfortable within themselves and in being alone. And I think that that's a very big problem for a lot of people is that they can't spend time alone comfortably.

The following exchanges in joint husband-wife interviews capture this sense of non-gregariousness in two couples:

I: OK. Do you get out during the day a lot? Do you go and visit neighbors or do you go shopping, to the store or something, or do you pretty much work right around here?

W: Right here.

I: OK. Do people. . . .

H: She doesn't socialize.

W: I'm the person to stay home. I don't like to visit and I don't. . . .

H: The only neighbors she'll visit are the people across the street.

W: I'm not social. I mean, once I get to know the person, like the girls I worked with at the mill . . . but as far as going out and actually visiting, I'm not that type of person.

And in another couple's comments:

W: Well, I wouldn't want to go out to work to socialize. I don't like going out to work. I like being home. I like to travel and things, but I like being home.

I: What do you think it is about being home that is so appealing?

H: Cause she is home. . . .

W: Yah, you know people who love to go to lots of parties . . . who just like to go, go, go all the time, and we like to go, well, we like to go fishing.

H: Our idea of getting out to do something away from home for recreational pursuits is that the two of us put the canoe on the car, go out to a pond and go fishing, maybe camp overnight down there if the kids are provided for, or even with the kids we'll go out. We've been camping or hiking or swimming. It's generally just something just as a family.

In interviews, then, twelve out of fifteen participants explicitly characterized themselves as non-gregarious, able to

work alone comfortably, not missing the socializing possibilities thought indispensable in the workplace. The remaining
three persons, who enjoyed socializing, were in public contact
jobs which provided socializing outlets.

Though participants clearly described themselves as non-
gregarious, I looked for other indications of this factor. The
demographic data sheet provided one such confirmation. To
the question, "List community memberships," responses were
quite sparse. Fifteen home workers and their spouses (a total
of thirty individuals) listed a sum of thirty-seven memberships, an average of 1.2 per person. Additional evidence for a
self-contained existence also came from reports on leisure
time activities. Reports on free-time usage invariably fell into
two categories: solitary activities (reading, oil painting, fishing, working up wood) or, more significantly, family-centered
activities (skiing, camping, traveling together). With a few exceptions, leisure activities involving membership in groups or
connections to external structures were absent. A list of cited
leisure time activities follows:

Free-Time Activities Reported by Home Workers

Activity	Number Citing
Reading	5
Gardening	4
Family games, play	4
Hunting, fishing	4
Traveling, relaxing with family	3
Needlework	3
Catch up on chores	3
Skiing	3
Cooking	2
Camping	2
Playing an instrument	2
Painting	1
Building furniture	1
Bicycling	1
Napping	1
Watching TV	1
Working on firewood	1
Raising animals	1
Stock car racing	1

The locus of leisure time, as reported, is plainly centered
within the workplace/home. Indeed, several people com-

mented on the apparent integration of some of their home and work activities:

> W: So for me the line between translating work and house-hold chores is not that sharply drawn. I mean, they are both work and they are in some ways enjoyable, but it's some-times either both feel more like work and sometimes they feel more like what I really want to do. . . .

> H: The garden—it's a hobby for some people. I mean, there may be pleasure in it. Jane gets a lot of pleasure out of the garden, but that's also part of our livelihood. . . .

Such a blending of leisure and work was also echoed by other respondents:

> H: I go to New York probably six or eight times a year now, and we (entire family) can all go. If I have to go to New York and I want to preview a couple of auctions we can all go to the previews at Sotheby's and Christie's. And while we are there we get to go to the Metropolitan Museum, we get to eat in its restaurant—and we get to do all kinds of things. You know, I mean, that's great. We all get to go to New York, it's fun. And the work part of it, it isn't grubby, dirty work—it's going to a nice place where there is 200 to 300 paintings hanging on the walls and you look at the paintings and that's your job. You're all done.

This same sense of integration of work and leisure is seen in other participants: the flytyer whose true avocation is fish-ing, the mechanic who enjoys stock car racing, the knitter who enjoys needlework activities, and the veterinarian who raises and shows fowl with his daughters. Although common-alities between work and leisure are not unique to this group alone, opportunities to incorporate leisure activities into the workday are. Time logs again reflected the integration of lei-sure and work activities during the day, as did observations. Moreover, these workers have the added opportunity to in-volve family members in both work and leisure activities, fur-ther blurring the work-leisure, work-family distinctions.

Non-gregariousness, it appears, supports the home worker in several ways. Primarily, it makes working alone in a non-social setting much easier and indeed even preferable; in-dividuals highly valuing the sociability of the workplace might be unhappy doing home work. Further, non-

gregariousness is consistent with the image of the autonomous worker. Secondly, it suggests a reorientation from
outside connections to familial sources for social interaction
and leisure time, demonstrated in the participants' stated
preferences for recreation. Certainly the combination of non-
sociable work settings and dependence on individual and
family for recreation suggests an intensified role for the family
in meeting the needs of the home worker. This more intense
family role is vitally expanded by looking at the role of spouses
in home work.

THE HOME WORKER AS A SPOUSE AND PARENT

Unlike traditional work-family studies, which deftly allocate
behaviors to one corresponding sphere or the other, isolating
the home work role from the family role is not as easily accomplished. Data from all sources—participant and spouse
interview, children's interview, observations and logs—attest
to the lack of sharp demarcation between work and family
roles for this sample. While most participants could offer an
estimate of hours spent working per week, thus meeting the
standard criteria for quantitative studies designed to compare
allocations of time to work or family, such cited time was pervaded by family interactions in a multitude of ways. Although
it would be inaccurate to say that home work life is unidirec-
tionally shaped by family concerns (just as earlier studies er-
roneously assumed the opposite), it is impossible to escape
the frequent interaction between the two systems. Some of
this interaction has been referred to in discussing the worker's individual characteristics (autonomy on the job to respond to family needs) but an examination of the spousal and
parental role underscores the existence of this relationship.
From the perspective of this sample, the emphasis is not on
how discrete or dichotomous the work-family relationship
is but rather on the extensive connectedness of loving and
working.

Focusing initially on the home worker and his/her spouse,
marriage to a home worker appears to propel the spouse into
the job situation. While the spouse whose husband or wife
works in a traditional, separate setting may participate in

that work vicariously through verbal report or social activities, work-at-home families in this study participated more directly. The spouse may be involved with the actual work operation, may provide the rationale for the choice of work style, may be called upon to enter into unanticipated child care and/or household duties, and/or intriguingly, may offer some support via his/her own somewhat non-traditional work style. Major aspects of the spouse's apparently inevitable involvement in home work are outlined below.

1. *Spousal Participation in Work*. Surprisingly, thirteen out of fifteen workers reported that their spouses were directly involved in their work. This involvement ranged from participating as a full-time worker (five spouses) to help with portions of the workload (eight spouses), even when the spouse held other outside employment. Most frequently mentioned assistance from the latter group included helping with bookwork, completing late tasks, dealing with the public, and handling odd jobs. Samples include:

> W: I'm well organized and I keep the books and records organized so I can tell him how many board feet he bought and what the price was so that he has a basis to make a decision. Just recently, for example, he was looking for some oak, and I thought, I think there was an ad in the paper and I cut it out and I stuck it some place in the office. I knew where it was and I was able to locate it, and that worked out. So I'm good at that kind of stuff—organizational stuff. I don't have any woodworking skill; neither do I have the interest.

And:

> W: But he (husband) can sit there and sew in some labels and poke a few threads, and you know, if he feels like picking up a sweater and working on it, he can do it.

Observations again played an important role in confirming reports of spousal involvement and capturing concrete instances of what that involvement entails, as in the following excerpts from observations:

> 10:00: Janet stands up, puts tools on shelf, takes down sewing machine. To her child she says, "I'm going to fold up some sweaters. Want to help me button?" Alice (3F), "No."

Janet goes over to get pile of sweaters which have been fin-
ished (husband John has sewed on buttons), buttons and
folds them for packing. She comments that John does about
one-third of the work by sewing on buttons. They talk about
readjusting work when Janet takes a three-week intensive
course: picking up the pace beforehand, John doing more of
the work, taking their daughter off for the day, etc. Janet
continues folding and packing sweaters, picking up dropped
stitches. Janet, John, and Alice talk back and forth, Alice
goes over to her mother, "I'm going to help button." She gets
a chair out, sits up to button, Janet: "You can help me look
for missing legs (on sheep on sweater pattern) too."

The following excerpt from observation in a veterinarian's
office illustrates themes of spouse involvement and responsiveness to family needs:

Woman #2 enters examining room. Mary (spouse) is there
too. Customer says dog needs a rabies shot, Mary and
Charles (veterinarian) tell her there's a rabies clinic in King-
field in the fall, then "She wouldn't have to bring him all the
way down." They attend to dog, phone rings, Mary answers
call about someone's dog in care, hooking phone over shoul-
der while helping to take dog off examining table. Lady waits
to pay, Mary interrupts phone conversation (about ordering
supplies) to tell women to bring other dog in. Charles is
cleaning examining room table, straightening counter. Mary
hangs up. Their own dog is visiting in examining room,
sniffing floor. Phone rings again, someone advised to come
get dog. "Can you come before 12:00? I'll be in and out of
the office this afternoon with dental appointments and mu-
sic lessons for the children."

Home work, then, appears to draw in spouses, regardless
of their own outside employment status. While the nature of
spousal participation varied both in degree and flavor, it is
doubtful that such a high rate of involvement (thirteen out of
fifteen) would be found among conventionally employed couples. Subtly or consciously, the presence of work in the home
for these families provided an opportunity for assisting and
sharing with a spouse's workload and a common ground for
mutual endeavor. Unlike most spouses who can participate
only vicariously, spouses of these home workers obviously
hold a concrete understanding of and involvement in their

partner's work. This is only one aspect, however, of the blurring of roles among home worker, spouse and parent.

2. *Spousal Participation in Child Care and Household Chores.* The nature and extent of men's and women's participation in household and child care chores has been a subject of lively interest and study over the past decade. Issues of who does what in the family have been propelled into prominence under the impetus of women's entry into the paid labor force. One branch of study has examined time allocations to household and paid labor in working families, while another has attended to the ideology supporting these choices. Few definitive conclusions have been reached, but Pleck (1979) suggested a grafting of these two branches of study in maintaining that new findings of increased household participation by men indicates that the ideology of social roles is changing, albeit slowly. He then theorized that the changing roles perspective may be plotted more carefully by studying "subgroups and innovative patterns" where roles may change at a different pace from larger segments of society; then, conceding that diversity exists, "a logical next step is to explore what factors appear to lead to a greater or lesser male family role. Of particular interest are attitudinal factors as well as demands from the work role" (Pleck 1979, 486).

Set against this background, work-at-home families have their own contributions to make to the study of work and family roles. Participants in this group reported high degrees of spousal participation in child care and household labor, in addition to the high measure of joint participation in the home work occupation: fifteen out of fifteen reported joint involvement in child care, and thirteen out of fifteen reported joint household labor. However, the nature of the spouse's employment affected the degree of participation, with conventionally employed spouses less able to devote as much time to this work as those who had more time flexibility. The spectrum of spousal involvement in household chores ranged from one housewife and one househusband at one end to two husbands working full time who were reported to perform minimal chores at the other. Strung out in between were spouses of home workers who performed substantial household chores both through report and observation within the confines of their outside job commitments:

Knitter describing her husband, a log truck driver:

> During spring break-up (ice out and mud season) when he
> is not working very much, he takes over the housework. . . .
> Sometimes I go through and he hasn't done a very good job
> of it, but you know, he does his best. He is real good with
> the kids. . . . Last week with that storm he was home—one
> day he was home all day and the other day he was home at
> three o'clock—and he got supper and he did the dishes and,
> you know, he helps a lot that way.

Due to the variety in their own working conditions,
spouses did not fall into any clear categorizations of chore involvement. The variety within the group and its small size
barred the generation of any conclusions about degree of
spousal involvement in househould chores. Their circumstances did permit a fruitful examination of the process of decision making about household chores. It is here that the
more interesting information about household labor emerged
as families found themselves in a state of negotiation and flux
on the topic. While five families reported clear divisions of labor along fairly traditional lines, the others mixed and alter-
nated who did what enough to place them in Pleck's
"changing roles perspective." Often these discussions and
changes were impelled by conditions of the work-at-home job.
This excerpt describes the process by which a knitter's home
work led to her husband's quitting his job at a wood mill and
becoming a househusband in support of her labor:

> H: Janet had so much work to do—looking after Alice, look-
> ing after the house, plus, like she said earlier, at least forty
> hours of work on the sweaters, even though she was doing it
> at home—which can be too much. I was getting very irrita-
> ble because I wasn't doing what I wanted to do in any way,
> shape, or form. So my staying home took the load off of
> Janet because I look after the house, I do the shopping and
> the cooking and whatever, and Janet can worry about the
> sweater end of it. It is working out much better this way.
>
> W: It reached the point where I would have to cut back on
> the amount of work that I was doing because I couldn't keep
> it up. At the beginning, there were slow times, and I didn't
> mind. I could take a lot of work for a couple of weeks. I could
> keep it up and I knew it would stop and I'd have a few weeks
> of nothing or relatively little to do, and that was fine. I could

do that. But when the business itself grew and I could have as much as I wanted, I couldn't keep it up for an extended period of time. So it was either cut back, or John would quit his job. It seemed so much more reasonable. John quit because it was very unhealthy in the wood mill as well as he was working nights and that disrupted. . . .

As the husband moved from the economic provider role into the househusband role, he also assumed some of the wife's work responsibilities, assisting with an estimated one-third of the knitting work.

This excerpt from a discussion between the chef-owner of a restaurant and his wife captures amusingly some of the ongoing negotiation over family roles influenced by work occurring in the home:

H: No, I just mean our family situation. I don't necessarily mean our work situation, but our family has become our business. I mean it's all so integrated that the other is impossible—it just doesn't exist.

W: What is the other?

H: The other is working somewhere and coming back and dinner is ready and you sit down and have a lovely dinner together.

I: In the very traditional sense.

W: And have a lovely dinner together prepared by me, too.

H: Yeah, yeah.

W: This was—until the last year or two when Peter finally gave up—I think the major, major, major source of conflict in our marriage, the fact that I didn't prepare our dinner. I don't know how it ever happened that I don't prepare dinners, but I don't prepare dinners for us. I've tried—I did try for a while and I was always in the way, which I had sort of been before when I tried because we don't have a place to cook upstairs (in their own living quarters). I have to cook down here and you have to cook from 4:00 to 6:00 which is the busiest part of the day.

H: If you had a kitchen upstairs, you still wouldn't cook. You're being unrealistic.

W: That's true, that's true.

H: You just don't cook.

W: How come we're having a kitchen made upstairs?

H: I don't know.

W: I think we ought to move the laundry back in there.

I: Should I turn the tape recorder off now?

H: (laughing) Oh this is mild, this is mild.

Simpler examples of similar role changes are captured in the following exchanges:

W: If I'm pushed for time, we have pizza for supper.

I: That sounds sensible to me.

H: Or I would cook.

And:

I: Do you find with the change of Todd working at home more that you are able to get more help from him with child care? Has his work—has it made it easier for you overall?

W: Yeah, different ways. When he wasn't home, we just didn't eat. When Nate was little and Todd wasn't home, I'd feed him real food, real meals, what children should eat, and I'd eat crackers and cheese or whatever because it was easier. But now we eat meals every meal, except some nights when we are too tired and they eat cereal and we eat pizza later. That way it has made more cooking and things like that.

I: That's an interesting observation. More demands on you.

W: More demands but, you know, he takes care of them, changes diapers if someone demands it and he cooks. Yes, and Friday is cleaning day because we can't clean the house much more than that. We kind of overlook a lot of it. One day a week is all we can stand. We all work on Friday till it's clean. One of us will take the upstairs and one the downstairs—so yes, he does help out if he's around.

I: So that is positive input then?

W: Oh, yeah.

I: As opposed to your having to be responsible not just for the child care but of all the cleaning.

W: No, he does a lot more in my job than I do in his.

The other families in flux or negotiation about household chores talked of leaving things undone until somebody was finally driven to do them, increasing children's participation, and "bumbling around during the day—doing whatever has to be done."

Whatever the specific dynamics of the individuals and families involved in the negotiating process, the significance of space as a contributor to this change must be reiterated. The intrusion of work into the homespace sometimes required renegotiation or merely facilitated it, as in the examples above. Apparently, spouses of these home workers are unable to ignore or hold themselves aloof from the repercussions of the home work occupation. In reverse, the intrusion of home into workspace allows the simultaneous performance of household and work chores revealed in logs and observations, for example, baking bread, doing a load of laundry, frosting a birthday cake. Lacking the separate safety of a distanced office or mill to assist in clearly demarcating family from work roles, shared space gives some indication of leading to shared roles.

Optimistic as this may sound, however, it needs remembering that women still bear the bulk of responsibility for household work and child care as indicated simply by the demographic consideration that women working at home have preschool children with them; further, women's reports in logs record more interspersing of work and household/child care duties than men's, and, of the six work-at-home men, three indicate that their wives carry the burden of household work while the other three share more equitably with their wives.

Attempting to extract a definitive conclusion about the nature of the relationship between home worker, spouse, and household/child care chores is impossible. However, tentatively, the following picture is suggested by the data: women may already have family needs in mind when they make the choice to work at home, unlike men. Therefore, they may see home work as a satisfactory arrangement through which they can reconcile the need to work with the need to fulfill parental/household duties. The ability to intersperse work and household duties through the day is perceived as preferable to the conflicts and stresses engendered by working conventionally. Autonomy on the job which allows response to family needs reinforces this attitude. However, their work situation apparently cannot be ignored by spouses who are inevitably drawn into work participation and, frequently, into child care and household tasks as permitted by their own work schedule. It may be that women request or demand this involvement but more likely the process is a subtle one building on the many daily and casual contacts between home and work demands.

For men working at home, the situation is somewhat cloudier, perhaps indicating the residual strength of stereotypes. Men tended to have a more separate work space rather than work within the family home, verbalize some need to separate work and family activities, and have older rather than demanding younger children. Three of these men were married to women who performed most of the traditional women's household chores while the other three participated more equally in househould labor. All of them, however, joined in child care, though again their children were older and less in need of constant attention.

3. *Nature of Spouse's Employment.* An unanticipated variable emerged from the demographic information on spouses' occupations. Strikingly, of fifteen spouses only three were conventionally employed. This means that twelve of the fifteen spouses were self-employed, worked at home themselves, were unemployed, or worked at a less-than-traditional forty-eight or fifty weeks-per-year job. The key characteristic of these spouses' non-traditional employment is that they all had a measure of time flexibility that could potentially respond to the home worker's schedule. Of the twelve spouses, five had entered into work with their home-working partner, and the remaining seven held jobs that were unconventional in the previously described conditions. Although there was no consistency across the nature and conditions of spousal occupations to allow for generalizations, several possibilities emerge for consideration. One is that marital homogamy exists—that independent, autonomous people marry individuals like themselves. Another is that being married to a spouse who is unconventionally employed provides a role model for attempting the same oneself. Another is that spouses might seek work opportunities which complement the home-

working spouse's ability to be flexible on the job to attain a mutual equilibrium. Whatever the specific reason, it is clear that some systems are interacting, that neither spouse's work or family role is totally independent of the other's.

Choosing a home work occupation seems to engender several changes in work and family lives. For most people, it is initially undertaken to allow more responsivity to children. However, its effects spill over into other areas of family life as it inevitably seems to influence the relationship between husband and wife. A sense of evening out of roles begins to emerge as home work demands renegotiation about small and large details, draws the spouse into the work system, spreads out household and child care chores, and apparently even affects the nature of the spouse's employment. This blurring of family-work boundaries occurs even with children, as the next chapter describes.

Chapter 6

The Children's View*

In fact, I thought about that, you know, about
how nobody is home after school and I would
hate that. I mean, I think that is terrible. I think
a parent should be there when the child comes
home from school. (A home-working father)

Well, we're probably a lot luckier because we can
see our parents. A lot of kids, their parents come
home, feed 'em dinner, and they're off again.
They don't get to spend much time with them.
(Twelve-year-old child)

Well, they're (home-working parents) not in such
a rush when you get home from school. Other
working parents don't have time for you. Like
Mom (a homeworker) gets us a snack and sometimes she sits down and watches television with
us. Parents that go out to work and come home
don't have really much time for their kids. (Nine-
year-old child)

C hildren provide the most direct impetus for seeking work-
family adjustments. Their arrival and presence stimulates
a host of changes ranging from the prosaic (can I get time off
to go to the school play?) to the profound (how much parental
time does a child need to develop healthily?). Introducing and
sustaining a child within a marriage relationship requires

---

*Portions of the information contained in this chapter appear in
Beach, B. "Children At Work: The Home Workplace" *Early Childhood Research Quarterly*, 3 (2), 1988, pp. 209–21.

major adaptations, but the child's ripple effect extends well beyond family boundaries. As parents grapple with the prosaic and profound details of integrating work and family commitments, the inherent contradictions between the two spheres are most harshly revealed. Childless workers who may have merely been occasionally inconvenienced by work demands become more seriously beset with the arrival of children who crystallize the complexities of balancing.

Given the lack of social and economic support for working families in the United States, responsibility for rearranging and choosing strategy falls on the individual family. If parental leave policies were universally mandated, then parents would not have to face the abrupt tug between nurturing the newborn and returning to the workplace. Were high quality, child centered day care readily and universally available, the horrendous difficulty of locating such care in a finite market would be eased. If employers more routinely offered and esteemed flexible work schedules, the impossible time conflicts between taking the child to the doctor and being at the workplace would be alleviated. If benefits such as sick child leave were employment options, then parents would not be caught in the crunch of missing work and/or searching for sick child care. Were alternative work patterns truly honored and respected, then parents could employ individual strategies most suitable to their needs. However, none of these supports are routinely available to most American families, so child care is a major flashpoint in work-family conflicts. Children thus become the nexus of the battle on both profound grounds (the emotional significance of parenting) and prosaic ones (the ongoing hassle of handling day care details).

What then happens when families choose a strategy of home-based work, deliberately electing to stray from conventional work paths? Are their frustrations lessened, or merely different? How does life change for children? Do their perceptions of their parents change? Families choosing this route commonly do so to mitigate the tension between working and nurturing, but there is precious little research on whether this is a meaningful, healthy choice for children. Because most research has focused on children as dependent variables, as outcomes of parental employment, we have only the weakest understanding of children's own perceptions of work and family interaction. Children in work-at-home families offer some remedy to that deficiency. Reported here are their perceptions and a sense of how those perceptions might fit in with a family strategy.

Recall, first, that parents (especially women) chose to work at home for family rationales, specifically the presence of young children ("I worked in the shoe shop eight years and five months. . . . And I knew I couldn't leave my kids. I cried every morning," "John and I didn't want to have a child and have someone else raise that child"). An intuitive sense of needing to be available to their children guided their decisions to elect working at home as one way of meeting both demands. Thus, the general context of receptivity to children was established. The emotional parameters of availability to children are difficult to discern but the pragmatic translation of availability was more readily observed. Quite simply, parents operationalized receptivity to children by permitting unrestricted space and time access. In contrast to the impenetrable, foreign culture of parental work for most American children, children in home-working families had easy, casual access to parental workspace. Thus, parents accomplished their goal of permitting more child-parent interaction by working at home. The effect of this work style did not stop there, however. True to a systems model, the children were not merely acted upon but also reacted to their parents' work. Sharing rather than separating work and family space and time distinctively flavored these children's perceptions of parental work in ways perhaps unanticipated by parents. As the results will show, children from an early age were familiar enough with their parents' work to describe it and to participate in it in developmentally appropriate ways. Further, children and parents were mutually involved in ongoing work socialization, a process in which twentieth-century parents customarily play a minimal role. Thus, from the simple wish to be more available to their children emerged a rather more complex model of parent-child interaction. In this model, children were indeed active rather than passive participants, a bold contrast to the usual children-as-outcome-variables approach. Following are the principal characteristics that emerged from the children's point of view.

KNOWLEDGE OF PARENT'S JOB

Without exception, every child old enough to be interviewed (twenty-four children, ages three to eighteen) could label his/ her parent's job, identifying it by a name or activity. The least forthcoming child (4F) reported "She knits" while more frequently elicited responses to the questions, "What does your mom/dad do all day?" described titles and functions:

"She sews sweaters, she works for Appleseed . . . or Copperberry" (sweater manufacturers) (3F).

"Translate. Changing one language into another" (10M):

"He ties flies, carves fish, does posters for people. He's a fisherman guide. He writes books" (8F):

"He sells tires. Changes oil, does grease jobs" (14M).

Further, when asked to delineate their parents' specific work activities, all children could list at least one procedure. An illustrative minimal response given by a three year old, naming only one procedure, was: "She sews on a machine— it's an old timer . . . it's an old machine and it has a dig-dag, dig-dag needle I think." Older children could offer a more complete description of what their parents did all day: "Mainly he's just like cooking bread or rice or something. And every afternoon he goes up for like an hour's nap because he's always working. Well sometimes he gets up at five o'clock and cooks straight through till two, sleeps for a while and then he comes in and starts the restaurant up" (12F).

The seven year old son of a day care provider described her work this way:

> She takes care of them (day care children) and tells them not to hit if they're hitting. . . . And she plays with the kids sometimes in the morning. And they had a plant once—a potato—and they put it in a dish with water and they let it grow and it's in that window. And it's very big now.

Responses to the question, "Does your mom or dad use any special tools or equipment on the job?" further reinforced the idea that children observe and understand their parents' work role. Asked to list tools or special equipment used by their parents on the job, the number of specific tools mentioned ranged from none to nine. Though one might anticipate very young children having the most difficulty in listing specific items, this proved not to be the case. The only children unable to respond were the five- and seven-year-old children of a day care provider; for them, a reasonable explanation might be that their mother's work and materials (toys) are so integral to their home as to be indistinct from their daily environment. (Their nine-year-old sister, however, volunteered that her mother's special equipment was "her hands.") All other children listed tools particular to their parents' work, with preschool and young children as capable of responding as older children.

Age, however, did prove to be a variable in the embeddedness of the response; that is, very young children were more likely to encapsulate their response in a meandering context. For example, in response to the question about tools or special equipment, a four-year-old boy with a woodworking father replied, "I don't use his chisels, too. Even I have some little screwdrivers. I have a new (work) bench too for Christmas."

And:

> (4M) He looks at mail . . . sometimes we open packages that come in the mail. Well you know what, one day Pa got a crate and he thought there were bricks inside it.
>
> I: Bricks! It must have been heavy. What was in it?
>
> C: It was a painting. It was made out of two-by-fours.

Age's influence on the context of responses reappeared in the general categorization of work and family roles. While all children were able to define their parent's job and/or work activities, preschool children were more likely to blend the two roles together in their responses. Illustratively, to the question, "What does your dad/mom do all day?" young children's responses included these:

> C (4M): Well sometimes he takes a bath. He sleeps most of the day.
>
> I: Uh-huh. Can you tell me anything else he does all day?
>
> C: Sometimes he works out in the gallery. . . .

A four-year-old said this about his father's work after initially describing his father's job correctly:

C: And he makes stuff for Jenny's house (toys to bring to the boy's day care home). He buys tar.

I: He buys what?

C: He buys tar. To put on the roof.

I: He buys tar for your roof. What else does he do all day?

C: Shovels the roof. Cause last week the roof, the shop roof was real heavy with snow so it would have fellen (sic) through.

By contrast, when school-aged children were asked to describe what their parents do, they, without exception, focused on job-related instead of parental or household activities:

I: Tell me what your mom does all day.

C: (15F) She usually wakes up at about the same time I do, which is about 8 o'clock or so; and she has to have half an hour to wake up, become totally aware of things. Then she usually starts at the sewing machine and I'm not exactly sure, exactly what she starts on like rainbows or cars or whatever. (The mother is a seamstress). I think she starts with big things because she's not so aware and it's easier to do big things in the morning than little tiny things that have jutty ins and jutty outs. And, around 11 o'clock she starts playing "beat the UPS man" and she rushes around the house, "Oh, help me—go downstairs and get a box," and I say, "Yes, mother deary." And bring upstairs a box and she rushes to get all the mobiles together and if the UPS man comes in at like 12 o'clock or something, she rushes around the house, "OH! OH! OH! OH!"

In assessing knowledge of parent's job, younger children had quantitative knowledge comparable to older children's as measured by their ability to identify the name, activities, and processes of the job. Significant qualitative differences existed in the contexts of their answers, however. Younger preschool children were much more likely to mention familial chores, to display egocentrism in their answers, and to blur the distinction between work and family roles. Older children attended to the work dimension and responded concretely to that role. This is entirely consistent with research in child development which demonstrates that children proceed from egocentric understandings to a broader perspective, including the ability to take other person's points of view. Very young children in these families understood that their parents were working and could describe many of those work processes, but did not discriminate between the parent and the worker role. For them, work existed, but it was a work which was readily responsive to the child's own needs, with parents interrupting, reconstructing, and shaping work needs to meet children's. The clear demarcation between worker and parent which divides the foreign work world from the intimate family one for most American children appears not to exist for these children. For them, integration implies a parent who works (clearly acknowledged by the children's ability to describe work) but who also blends and fulfills parental duties as needed. No artificial distinction between worker and parent is present in a setting which encourages child-parent interaction during the work day, a setting created and sustained by parental choice.

INVOLVEMENT IN WORK

Displaying knowledge of parental work is not simply a nicety, unrelated to any other dimensions of the work-family connection. The concrete knowledge of parental work demonstrated by all the children in the study formed a base from which they moved into participation in their parents' work. Quite subtly but inevitably children moved from simply watching their parents work to assisting with it in progressively age-appropriate ways. This lengthy and natural process was unanticipated by parents, who were not coercing their children but simply responding to their interests, just as any parent, for example, allows a child to help with sweeping or dishwashing. In such an unforeseen manner, parents extended their availability to their children beyond the parental role to incorporate children into their worker role as well. Thus the work-at-home context both informed children about their parents' work and broadened their understanding of their parents as workers by involving them in the work process.

One way to understand parental work is to observe it; a second is to assist in it. Clearly, the nostalgic ideal of parents and children working together in collective unity (if such an historical condition ever did exist) has been usurped by twentieth-century public education. Time required by school is a major constraint on children's available time to work alongside parents. General fear of child labor laws is another concern voiced by home-working parents; as one parent stated, "I'm real careful with it—these things that have been going on about child labor—you know, I think about that." Despite such restrictions, all children in the sample were involved to some degree with their parents' work. The involvement ranged from help with simple household and work tasks to one twelve-year-old who worked thirty hours per week as underchef in a family restaurant. Some work was remunerated, some was not. Some work was regular and some fluctuated with season or need. All children aged three or older helped with household chores in support of their parents' work both through self-report and parental report. Essentially, the data obtained from children in interviews suggested the following scheme of help. This initial scheme was amplified by observational data, examples of which are cited:

Levels of Involvement
1. Play/watch/help
2. Simple tasks
3. Assistance with work on a regular basis, paid or unpaid
4. Regular paid work

Level 1—Play/watch/help. Rather than being a catchall category to describe very young children's involvement, it became apparent through observation and interview that this was a necessary precursor to later, more meaningful involvement. The mechanism by which children become socialized to work is imprecisely known, but the opportunity to watch weighed heavily in this sample, so there was not always a clear distinction between Level 1 and Level 2. For example, one twelve-year-old girl who chops vegetables and garnishes for her family restaurant on a regular paid basis now describes her gradual introduction to using sharp knives through observation.

C: Sometimes when he's (dad) boning the veal and we have nothing to do cause we don't have TV, we just sit and watch him. . . . Then halfway through December on a slow night, I came into the kitchen, I was watching him and he started to show me how to do stuff (chop vegetables).

I: The knives must be sharp—how did you learn to use them?

C: We've been using sharp knives since we were real little, cause we were always watching my dad and stuff.

Her father's remembrance in interview verifies her own memory:

I: When would she have started observing you in the kitchen or becoming aware?

H: As soon as she could sit up.

W: She was nine months old.

I: When she first sat in the kitchen?

H: Yeah. So she has picked up from there.

I: So she has become qualified as a reasonably skillful assistant cook by virtue of having the opportunity to watch you.

H: Just viewing.

Another longitudinal example of a child's evolution from observing/playing to regular paid employment is offered by this veterinarian father whose daughter started accompanying him on occasional barn rounds at six months:

So Lori would go along and ride in the truck. And if I was going in the barn I would take her in with me and I would set her in the hay and leave her so she'd be out of the way, particularly if we were going to have to catch a calf or something like that.

This twelve-year-old daughter can now hold barn animals giving birth as well as assist with C-sections in the office.

That children play/watch their parents work from an early age was underscored by observations. The youngest child in the sample, a seven-month-old when I first observed him, was present in his mother's beauty shop while she worked. At various times she gave him pink curlers to play with; held him up to the large shop mirror to play; held him in her lap and spun him around in the barber chair; sat him up under the dryer as it blew cool air; handed the baby a shop towel to play with; and watched as customers cooed and played with him.

Every observation I did while preschool children were present revealed those children playing/watching in some capacity, whether playing with scraps of yarn or cloth, needles or tools for a knitting machine, or the paper punch for a secretary. The following vignette from the observation of a home knitter and her two-year-old daughter reveals the very small, ordinary incidents upon which knowledge and involvement are built at a very young age:

> Karen (2F) still watching, walks behind her mother's chair, yawns. Mo: "Still tired?" Karen: "Yeah." Karen watching mother thread needles, approaches very close to watch intently. Mo: "Get back, you'll get your eye poked." K: "I want that" (three-pronged tool). Mo: "No" Karen: "Yes" Mo: "No" Karen touches needles. Karen: "Daddy knit?" Mo: "No" Karen: "Mommy knit?" Mo: "Yes" Karen starts to play with needles. Mo: "Don't touch," she warns again. "I'm gonna get ugly." Karen moves end needles (on machine), "I want that." Mother is doing hand work to pick up dropped stitches. Karen leaves needles alone, picks up heavy sweater weight, stands and plays with it. Mo: "Watch it, don't drop it on your toes." Karen balances weight across arms. Mo: "What's on TV in the other room? It sound like a baby." Karen: "See" and runs into other room, runs back and says "Cartoons." picks up weight again. Mo: "Be careful with that" then "No! Now leave it on the floor." Karen picks up machine guard, mother takes it from her and replaces it. Mo: "Out! You want to go get back up on the couch?" Karen picks up punch card (for sweater pattern), comes over to show it to me. "Holes," pointing to the card, "Mommy's," "everywhere." Mother spills cup of tools, Karen runs over to help pick up. Mother removes sweater from machine, holds it up. Karen: "Sweater." Karen asks for ties on pants to be tied again. Mo: "If you're not going to watch TV then go shut it off," several times. Karen: "No, cartoons." Mo: "Then go watch it," all the while finishing up sweater and then places it on play table. Karen goes over as mother restokes stove, picks up sweater and holds it appropriately by shoulders, "See?" "See? It fits me" as she holds it in front of her, then ties arms around her waist, "See?"

Cumulatively, such ordinary, trivial, and sometimes exasperating encounters construct a fundamental basis for the child's later involvement with work. Playing/watching underlay most children's subsequent work experiences. It is not remarkably unique that most children should want to be near or involved in their parents' activities—children of at-home mothers have done this for years. What is distinctive is the presence of work in the child's immediate space, affording him/her an entry usually denied to children.

Level 2—Simple tasks. There is no firm demarcation between Levels 1 and 2; often children in the initial stages of watching slip imperceptibly into helping with simple tasks, such as the aforementioned child who picked up her mother's spilled knitting tools. Simple tasks related to work occur casually during the course of work, are irregular in nature, and are not crucial to work's completion, though they may be helpful. Following are some examples in response to the question asked children, "Do you ever help him/her out when she's/he's working?"

> C (9F): Well, I, when she goes out to milk I have to babysit MaryAnn (a day care child) sometimes and other times, well, I'll have to keep an eye on the day care kids. . . .

And:

> C (3F): Umm, umm, when she had a lump in her body . . . (turns to mother) where were you hurt?
>
> Mo: Hip.
>
> C: When she hurt her hip I passed her her sweaters in bed.
>
> I: That would be a real help.
>
> C: And I passed her her sweatshirt and she read me stories . . . and (regarding the sewing machine used to hem sweaters) I pop it (thread) into the little hole for Mommy and then I put it through the holes in the sewing machine.

And:

> C (7M): He sells the tires. I roll them over to him sometimes.

And:

> C (9F): Well, sometimes I help her find a tool when she loses them.
>
> I: OK.

C: Oh, yeah, I help her take the yarn out of her sweaters.

I: That's a pretty big help I would think.

C: I help her ravel it up on that wheel thing, whatever you call it.

Observations in each home confirmed these examples given by children, that is, I saw each of the cited children performing that or a similar task. However, it merits emphasis that such tasks were of a spontaneous nature and occurred when the child was present incidentally; none of these children in Level 2 was continuously involved in their parents' work. These children had voluntarily interrupted their play to join their parents, or just happened to be present when the parent made a request for help. These simple tasks of Level 2 were most frequently performed by young elementary school children, aged six to eight.

Level 3—Assistance with work on a regular basis, paid or unpaid. This stage is distinguished not by pay or hours worked (neither of which is uniform across this sample) but by regular involvement in the parent's work of a meaningful nature, beyond the casual simple tasks. While not critical to the completion of the job—that is, the parent could accomplish these jobs—children involved at this level provide some time release to the parent, freeing him/her up to complete other parts of the job. These children display knowledge of the job's process and sufficient skill to perform parts of it independently. Examples here include:

C (14M): I help change tires. I answer the phone sometimes. . . . Oh yeah, I wash windows and vacuum out the cars.

And:

C (12F): I clean and I hold the animals. I hold up the dogs when they stand on the table. I get medicine, I sell things once in a lifetime. . . . I've helped with the baby puppies.

And:

C (10F): Yeah, yesterday I was writing out cards for him, he said I had to write down the name of a fly, "Blue Smelt," and then on the top write the number "8."

I: Do those cards go with each package of flies?

C: Well, the fly gets stapled onto the card and then you put it in a little bag.

I: Do you ever do the stapling and bagging too?

C: Sometimes.

I: Do you think you could ever tie flies if you needed too?

C: Yeah. Because he's taught me, like the first fly I tied was a "Royal Coachman."

Level 4—Regular paid work. Finally, two children (18F and 12F) work regularly for pay for their parents, contributing substantially to the job's completion. In both cases, other people would typically have to be paid to fulfill the child's work load. Another child (12F) moves into a similar capacity during summer vacations. Eighteen-year-old Carol participates in cottage knitting with her parents, performing varying amounts of work depending on her schoolwork schedule. A skilled knitter herself, she can finish and sew almost all the designs her family works on. As her mother says:

> W: Now my youngest daughter, she—unless she's doing her homework—cannot go in the living room and just sit down in a chair and watch TV. She'll just automatically say, give me a needle and reach over and get some work and start. . . . She does more now overall on helping than she did when I was—you know—like I'd give her this pile that she had to do and she knew that if she did those ten sweaters that she had $10. Well, now with her just setting there and taking whatever she wants to work on, she'll do more and earns more than she did before.

PROCESSES OF CHILDREN'S ROLE

Assessing children's knowledge and involvement in their parents' work through measurement of tools mentioned, interactions observed, knowledge of functions, etc., is a relatively simple task grounded firmly in tangibles. As such, they provide simple, graphic indicators of integration. More elusive to gain is a comprehension of the processes by which children develop these understandings, for the easily observable prosaic details are rooted in the emotional interaction of parent and child. Since processes are inherently longitudinal, developmental, subjective, and/or invisible (or a combination of the four), they are infrequently handled by social scientists. Yet it is vital to address how and why children develop understandings of work and work-related behaviors, in order to fill in the missing steps in the pathways from independent to dependent variables. Children in work-at-home families, engaged in the reconciliation of two powerful social systems, offer a unique group with which to start the search. Further, the small amount of existing literature attending to occupational socialization of younger children acknowledges the hypothetical significance of parents as role models for identification or sources of personal contact about occupations but leaves unexplored the specific connections between parent-child-work. Regardless of the inherent complexities, the processes by which children develop understandings about work deserve exploration for it is obvious that children's work involvement ties in with the broader theme of integration in meaningful ways.

Approaching process required combining methodologies again. While interview provided much helpful background, observations both crystallized themes from interviews and offered a view of very subtle activities often not mentioned in interviews. Mounting evidence from observations clarified some important hallmarks of this process, and lent substance to critics' demands for more attention to the connectedness of working and loving rather than the discontinuities.

Again, utilizing time and space as analytical tools proved fruitful. How families allocated time and space to children vis-a-vis work illuminated quite plainly the connections of working and loving. While for conventionally employed parents work time and work space are impenetrable barriers to their children, the easy access of children to their home-working parent's space and time again set the stage for interaction with the work process.

First, and most obvious, space facilitated the interaction needed for process to occur. As noted earlier, in eight of the homes work and family space were overlapping—living rooms, kitchens, dining rooms—while in seven homes there were separate work spaces devoted exclusively to the occupation though still a part of the home. This physical distinction did not extend to access rules, however, as in no home was work space forbidden to children. Children thus had the opportunity to interact almost unreservedly with their parents because access was so available. Parents both verbalized this accessibility in interview data and displayed it during observation. For example, an art dealer said in interview that his two preschoolers are welcome to join him in his gallery: "When I'm working I don't mind if Nate brings his toys in— when I'm writing some letters or something—Nate and Sarah will often play in the same room." On both of my subsequent observations, the normally dignified gallery was enlivened by a rocking horse, Legos and other playthings scattered on the floor and both children were indeed playing while their father was calling Sotheby's on the telephone.

A similar comment, indicating receptivity to children, is made by a knitter:

> W: I'm there, I can stop—some people have to really concentrate and if they are interrupted, it really bothers them. I can stop right in the middle of it and you know, untie a knot or whatever needs to be done, they'll bring it to me. . . . And then I can go right back to what I'm doing and not make mistakes, you know. . . . A lot of times they sit right in there at the table and do puzzles or something. . . . And it doesn't bother me. I can see why it would some people, you know, but I've been doing it for two years and I have learned all the things that you have to check before you make another step and my eyes will dart around and look at 'em and I know that I am not going to go across and it's going to fall on the floor.

Observations substantiated both parents' and children's comments about access to work space. In all situations where children were present during the workday, they were in and out of the work space, sometimes helping or sometimes seeking personal attention. It became apparent, however, that children had become socialized to their parents' work expectations—though access was unrestricted, it appeared to be rarely abused. Several parents commented that children "knew" when they were working and needed to be uninterrupted. In some situations it appeared that parents had, over time, verbalized to children what was expected of them, often in very mundane ways: "Sometimes I get irritated if they want me to get up and go get 'em a drink, and I'll say, 'Get it yourself.' They've got two feet." Other parents took the time to give lengthier explanations, as seen in this observation:

> Father continues writing at desk, Nate (4M) sits quietly in chair, then jumps up and runs behind sofa, giggles.
>
> Father: "Nate, why don't you find something to do? You can do it in here if you want, just find something to do." Nate runs out of gallery, father says "I hate losing my place when I'm adding something—her we go for the third time!" (Nate returns with a punch out book which needs adult assistance).
>
> Father: I can't help you right now."
>
> Nate: "Why don't you want to help me now?"
>
> Father: "You guess."
>
> Nate: "Because you're working."
>
> Father: "Right."
>
> Nate: "Why are you working?"
>
> Father: "Because I have to. Do you know today is June first and I have to do last month's books. I'm adding up these figures and making a bank deposit slip. I have to make a phone call, there's a letter from Antiques magazine about our ad I have to answer, I've got to check over the mail for letters I have to answer. So you'll have to choose some other toy."
>
> Nate: "How long is this going to take?"
>
> Father: "About an hour and when I'm on the phone please be quiet."

In this situation, space access allowed the preschool child a detailed explanation of what "work" was for his father at that time. Not all children received such explicit verbal description though space access enabled all children to obtain, minimally, visual understanding of their parent's work.

More explicit instruction about work values occurred in shared space as well. While parents generally might endorse certain work values to their children, work space access in the home allowed the child to observe his/her parent demonstrating desired behaviors and to receive verbal instruction appropriate to the task at hand. Expression of these values emanated not from interviews as much as from observations; for example, part of an observation of father and sons depicts both direct instruction in procedure as well as reminders of necessary behavior:

> They (father and two sons ages seven and fourteen) are mounting a new tire. As father checks pressure, Son #1 (14M) removes screw holding tire in place, replaces it in holder. Father puts newly mounted tire on air machine to check for leaks as Son #1 lifts second old tire, places it on rim machine and using machine separates tire from rim. Son #2 (7M) is watching throughout, balancing on new tire, rolling it. Son #1 uses wedge to remove tire totally from rim, starts up wire brush machine to clean rim again as father hammers lugs in first tire, son rolls it out and gets ready to mount it on wheel. Son #1 to #2: "Go get Daddy the air gun." Son #2 goes out, picks it up from one side of the truck and brings it to dad who uses it to mount tire. Son #2 returns to watch brother who is working on rim. Father returns, "Get it?" and shows Son #1 how to put sealer on. "To get that stuff on, you gotta put it right up here," then finishes job. Son #2 picks up sealer brush and runs it on inside edges of new tire. Father to Son #2, "OK, all done up son?" and lifts tire onto rim as he and son #2 mount it on rim. Father fills it with air from compressor, checks pressure with gauge, accidentally drops air hose which Son #2 picks up and hands to him. Father to Son #1: "Where'd you put those caps?" and reminds him of proper place to put them so they don't get lost—"they cost ten cents a piece."

Another observed example of direct instruction in work behavior is depicted in this example in a family restaurant:

> 5:05 Lisa (12F) comes in from outdoors.
>
> 5:10 Father returns from upstairs.
>
> Lisa: "Why did you want me back so early?" (she's been at a friend's). He explains that "We're open at 5:00. What if somebody came up the driveway right now? They don't care if

you're at Julie's." Reminds her of need to be ready to work at 5:00 (regardless of when first party actually arrives). Then he says, "OK, let's get this place cleaned up and ready."

Such brief fragments indicate examples of socialization in process—through direct instruction, through modeling by the parent, and through child's observation of work processes. A hallmark of these encounters was their naturalness, facilitated by casual access to work space. Thus, parents were not reduced to lecturing abstractly but could tie desirable behaviors to the concrete work setting accessible to the child. These examples are encompassed within "role model" but lend specificity to that vague concept. W. Moore (1973) indirectly theorized that children in such families may internalize work appropriate norms more readily than their counterparts who lack access to their parents' work when he emphasized the significance of affect in occupational socialization:

> The hypothesis is that normative internalization takes place only in situations marked by strong affectivity in relationships. . . . This is not a very radical idea in view of our knowledge of the importance of response to the expectations of significant others, but it does serve to caution against much "character-building" to emerge from formal admonition. (Moore 1973, 869)

The second analytical tool for approaching process, time, proved again to be more complex than space. Time, like space, was generally accessible to children, and worktime did not exclude children from receiving parental attention. To the contrary, worktime was often structured around children as previously noted. However, it quickly became apparent that adult concerns about time (quality vs. quantity, how to allocate it, work time vs. play time, etc.) were not applicable to children. From a child's perspective, time boiled down to one simple metaphor: availability of parent to child. Though one might expect preschool youngsters to be demanding of parental time for themselves, the strongest voicing of the need for parental availability came surprisingly from school-aged children who had some perspective from friends on what it might mean not to have parental access. Thus, age again played an important mediating role in how time was conceptualized by children, though underlying all ages' conception of time was parental availability.

The presence of preschool children was frequently cited by parents as a motivation for choosing to work at home. Consequently, a reasonable expectation was that preschoolers would be listened and attended to during worktime rather than being shut out. This proved to be a logical assumption. Preschool-kindergarten children were present in thirteen observations and only rarely was a child-initiated overture rebuffed. Recollecting the data reported earlier, preschool children received 8.30 tends by adults per two-hour observation period; school-aged children received 2.71.

Outright refusals were non-existent—no parent ever refused a request for time or access, (for example, "No, I won't talk with you now,") and the few rebuffs observed were couched in explanatory terms. For example:

9:05 C (4F) leaves table (where mother is working) to kitchen. "I want peanut butter."

Mo: "Just a minute. I'll be there as soon as I finish cutting."

The presence of preschool children virtually guaranteed time interruptions for response to questions and conversation, as well as simple requests for help. Most parents managed to work and respond simultaneously:

Janet is busy picking out dropped stitches, "Another mess." She fills out more irregular cards, "I'm not exactly hurtling along. Stopping for this mess is time consuming." Moves onto next sweater. Alice (3F) comes to show Beauty Bear— Janet says Alice is into rhyming—talks with Alice about Sesame Street rhyming characters. Alice talks to mother about picture she has drawn, mother responds as she sews. John (father) drives off to work in woods as Alice watches, deciding not to go. Janet talks about Alice and John building a log structure for turkeys. Alice shouts across field to father as mother sews. Alice returns to mother's side, talks with mother about chicken raising, broilers eaten by foxes—asks mother more about broilers, "Broilers is a silly name." Alice asks about "stampers." Mother: "I don't understand that word," as she sews. Back and forth discussion. Alice sits in rocker at mother's side, talking with her as she sews. 9:25

Sewing, chatting continue. Mother mentions ease of talking and sewing, but not thinking deeply and talking. She and Alice talk about one time she injured her finger with needle, going to hospital, other family injuries. Alice asks questions answered by her mother, "What is blurred?" "Was my nose running?" Much back and forth talk. Alice runs to door to look across field at father working, runs back to sit in rocker and chat. Sewing continues amid general chat. Alice asks questions about Santa Claus, vocabulary words, house design, all of which are answered by mother.

Or a simpler illustration:

(Mother of Anna (4F) and Jane (6F)—machine knitting).

Anna makes baby sounds, mother laughs while knitting. "Are you a baby Anna?"

Anna: "Where's Daddy?"

Mother: "He's hauling a load of wood. (Discusses for whom).

Jane approaches machine with school papers, mother pauses to look it over and help her with it (2 minutes), resumes knitting.

Anna: "How do you spell 'zoo'?"

Mother: "Z-o-o"

Anna: "How do you spell 'zebra'?"

Mother: "Z-e-b-r-a"

For all parents observed, when a problem arose work was set aside and the child attended to:

(Mo. stuffing a crib mattress at table)

2:20 Darcy (4F) comes to table, "Is my Uncle James a cowboy?"

Mo: "Cowboys don't just ride horses. They also take care of cows—your daddy's a cowboy."

Darcy scrapes her carrot on the table, mother asks her to stop. "NO!" Darcy drops some paper on floor, needs to be coerced into picking it up, and then wants some hugging. She sits in her mother's lap, hugs, they make up. Darcy looks at mattress fabric, "Those are pretty flowers. What are they?" Mother: "Rosebuds." They look at other leaves and flowers, talk about colors. Mother says, "If you go find a short book, I'll read it to you. A short one." (They read for the ensuing twenty minutes).

Parents' ready integration of preschool children into their worktime—their ability to respond and work simultaneously, to interrupt or even neglect their work when necessary— needs to be understood in the context of their willingness to do so. A "system" is clearly operating here: that children see their parents as readily available to them because parents, on their part, have chosen to be so and have elected a work structure enabling this availability. This is obviously a key to why preschoolers blended their descriptions of parent and work roles, for the environment created for them by their parents is devoid of family-work role dichotomies that more typically prevail. Time for preschoolers is a fluid access to parents without the constraints imposed by external work schedules on most children's parental access. For this reason, when asked to describe their parents' day, they are as equally likely to cite family activities as work activities.

Time as a metaphor for parental availability was most strikingly verbalized by elementary school aged children. Although most parents feeling pressure to balance work and family life are immediately impelled by the presence of very young children, this study found elementary school children to be unexpectedly vocal about the benefits of parental access. The question "How does it feel to have a parent working here instead of at a factory or an office?" elicited nearly unanimous response; eleven of the thirteen elementary school children immediately volunteered answers revolving around parental availability to them:

> C (9F): Well, they're not in such a rush when you get home from school. They're not really . . . they (other working parents) don't have time for you. Like Mom, she gets us a snack and sometimes she sits down and watches television with us. Parents that go out to work and come home don't really have much time for their kids. And they have to leave in the morning so they get ready and go and say goodbye and they let their child go out to school but she (mother) waits in that window where we get on the bus so she can talk with us while we're waiting for the bus. And it's neat that she has more time.

Other children volunteered similar availability themes:

C (9F): I like it. I get to see my mother a lot, and I like to see my mommy and she stays home with me a lot. When I come home I can just say "Hi, Mom."

C (6F): Well, when I come home I feel that I can talk with her, that she's there when I need her.

C (10M): I don't really think about it, but it feels good. . . . I like it a lot better than if they were in some office all day. . . . (Because) they're there when I'm there.

C (12F): Well, we're probably a lot luckier because we can see our parents. A lot of kids, like their parents come home, they feed 'em dinner, and they're off again. They don't get to spend much time with them.

Such statements exemplified the positive feelings about parental availability among elementary school aged children. Several children went on to include negative statements about babysitting:

C (9F): I have another answer. I don't like going to babysitters. So I could stay home all day—(if sick, for example) I don't like going to babysitters.

C (9M): Good. You don't need to be babysitted. You can do what you want . . . babysitters don't know what your mother lets you do and you can't do what you are used to.

C (8F): Sometimes people just have babysitters, because their parents are both out at the same time and you don't get to see your parents—sometimes those other kids don't.

No other category of answer existed to the question, "How does it feel . . . ?" Every response given was couched in terms of parental availability. While school-aged children may be receiving information from their parents about the desirability of parent being home, it is apparent they are also drawing their own conclusions based on observations of their friends at school, and/or earlier babysitting experiences of their own.

Nor was parental availability a figment of their imaginations. Coincidentally, four observations occurred as elementary school aged children arrived home. In all four cases, parents laid aside their work to spend a few minutes talking with the child about their day, preparing a snack and relaxing informally. In interview, parents generally confirmed this pattern: that work was interrupted or completed for the day as children arrived home from school:

> And if I have bookwork to do or rebillings of people who haven't paid or this type of thing, I try and do that before they get home from school so that I'm done generally by 3:00, 3:30 at the most (Mother).

> I honestly believe that the boys are a little—what do I want to say—a little more content, too, you know, to come home and find a parent home, 'cause every night the first thing they do when they get off the bus, they come to the garage door and open up the door and, "Hi, Dad!" (Father).

This pattern of parental availability to school-aged children appeared also on the daily logs where interruptions of work due to arrival of children were duly noted.

For the three teenagers in the study, parental availability figured importantly.

> C (15F): Her (mother) being home during the summer instead of not being home and being home as soon as I get home and, it's, I get more of a chance to air my feelings, instead of keeping them bottled up inside of me at a babysitters—just the noise and tension getting to me and making me nervous, expanding to even bigger ones—I can just come right home, and it seems, ah, it brings me more close somehow.

Teenagers also indicated specific tangible benefits of their parents' working at home: source of transportation (especially vital in a rural area), help with school homework, availability to bring forgotten items to school, and better supervision.

Thus, for all age groups, time proved to be a key analytical tool. Children's perception of time readily translated into parental access, albeit with developmental differences: for preschoolers, it meant simultaneous and spontaneous integration into work and family activities; for elementary school children it indicated parental availability to them especially in arrival home from school; and for teenagers, general availability for emotional and logistical support. Interestingly, most parents' expressed motivation for working at home was to be available to very young children; however, it appears from children's interviews and observations that parental access remains crucial to the relationship long after the preschool years.

Returning to the introductory concept of process of learning about work, it is apparent that family allocation of time and space unite to create a distinct environment. Based on data, these distinguishing features include:

1. A work setting free of the conventional physical and temporal barriers to family access.

2. Corresponding children's utilization of that access.

3. Opportunity to observe parental work and consequent knowledge about tools and activities of parental work.

4. Opportunity for involvement in parental work at all ages in developmentally appropriate ways.

5. Exposure to socialization in work activities and behaviors through observation, involvement, modeling, and direct instruction, all in an atmosphere of affectivity and informality.

6. Development in a non-dichotomous work-family setting and consequent recognition of the connections between working and loving.

What, then, can we learn from these twenty-seven children about the illusory concept of integration? What role can they play in substantiating an intuitive yearning by working parents to be more responsive to their children? What do the homely details of their daily lives offer in comprehending an overarching abstraction?

Vitally, these children's experiences ground us in the reality of integrating on a daily basis. Most working parents, expressing guilt, stress, and inadequacy, want to be vaguely more adaptable to their children's needs but lack a coherent, pragmatic sense of what that adaptability entails. Work-at-home families, having elected one such strategy for balancing, offer a view of what daily responsiveness to children involves. Parents choose the context of availability by working at home, and children fill in the details by moving unrestrictedly between work and family space and time, by demanding responses which interrupt the parent's work schedule, by ob-

serving and then participating in their parents' work, by becoming partners in a work socialization process, by verbally
appreciating their parents' availability and thus reinforcing it,
and by creating a relationship very much rooted in the connectedness rather than separateness of loving and working.
Drawing children into the work relationship rather than rul-
ing them out creates a unique blend in which dichotomizing
or segregating becomes impossible.

These twenty-seven children also help correct a longstanding deficiency in the study of children and work. Ro-
bustly, through numerous prosaic encounters, they assist in
developing a sense of children as initiators, actors, activists
in the family-work relationship. Rather then simply being
outcome variables, they provide input into the work-family
equation by asserting a role for themselves, demonstrating
the small contributions which cumulatively reshape broader
social roles. For example, their parents' daily work schedules
little resemble conventional work patterns as they seek to
adapt to children's needs; thus, the parent's fulfillment of role
as worker diverges from common social definitions of that
role. Further, as children observe and then participate in
their parents' work, they become mutually involved in redefining the parental role. Unlike most parents, for whom socializing a child for work is no longer a parenting function,
these parents actively and intimately assume a principal role
in their children's socialization for the world of work. Not only
are these parents resuming a role discarded in the nineteenth
century, when work was removed from the home, but they are
offering what seems to be a gender neutral process as children, both boys and girls, display knowledge of and participate in the parents' work, be the parent male or female.

Finally, these children offer a chance for prospective integrators to evaluate thoughtfully the reality such a work style
implies. Being more available or responsive to children is a
fine abstract goal but the daily reality of that responsivity may
simply be unacceptable to some parents. For home-working
families (admittedly perhaps at the most extreme end of the
integration spectrum), responsivity to children entailed frequent work interruptions often of a trivial nature, as meeting
child care needs could be exasperating at times. Parents who
would not find the kind of child care interactions portrayed

here to be rewarding would perhaps best reconsider their options. Only rarely are interactions with children profound from the adult point of view, and the parent who finds this responsivity taxing should perhaps carefully examine his/her concept of integration.

Chapter 7

Accommodating Work and Family

Thus far, home work convincingly demonstrates how a family system might operate. Spouses, children, and workers themselves encounter the work system, assimilate it in ways useful to them and accommodate to it where necessary. Overall, home workers display more power to remold and recast work demands to fit family needs than do conventionally employed workers, standing as they do at the center of the work-family intersection. For most workers, the structured rules of the workplace dominate the center of work and family life, providing a pattern to which families must mold themselves, rather than the reverse. For potential integrators, negotiating this interaction between work and family life represents the greatest challenge since most workplaces offer little material for malleability. The flexibility of space and time in home working families, the sense of autonomy to respond to family needs experienced by home workers, and the casual access and involvement of other family members provide a conspicuous contrast with most work environments. For these families, the work system and the family system perhaps weigh more equally, with the balance often tipping in favor of the family.

Cumulatively, the interactions we have seen enlarge the scope of integration beyond the pairs involved. Individually, the interaction of home worker and work, spouse and worker, child and worker, for example, are all indices of some measure of integration, of pulling together work and family roles. Graphic examples of integration provided by these families— the child assisting with parental work, the intermingling of work and family space—lend some tangibility to a nebulous concept. Important and useful as these examples of interacting dyads are, however, they do not represent the sum of what integration can reckon for a family. Beyond these graphic examples extends a widening ripple of integration which spills its effects into family dynamics. Some of these effects may be anticipated and welcomed, while others might be unexpected and less than desirable. The following sections examine the nature of some of these whole family effects.

FAMILY RESULTS: ADAPTABILITY

The essence of a systems perspective of the family is that the family unit is more than the sum of its parts. Although it has been possible to tease out characteristics particular to individuals or dyads in reporting results, there is a second order level of effects which deals more with the family entity than with pair relationships. Some of these systemic categories emerged from interviews but observations more graphically and realistically developed them, again suggesting the value of incorporating direct observation in research design. Findings from family results here reaffirm the value of direct observation in understanding families' lives, although such observation is not frequently utilized by family researchers.

From interviews emerged the participants' perceived autonomy to respond to family needs described several sections earlier. Observations reinforced, extended and amplified this theme, moving the focus from the individual's perceived autonomy to a sense of family adaptations enabled by the home work job. Interviews placed the initial focal point of this responsiveness in the worker him/herself but observation created more of a sense of family adaptativeness to newly arisen circumstances, some trivial, some major. A modest example is the sick child: for conventionally employed parents utilizing out-of-the-home day care, a sick child represents an emergency, usually necessitating absence from work through use of personal or sick leave days (Kamerman 1980, 94–95). One observation happened to occur on a day when a child was home sick from school and displayed, by contrast, how minor an issue child care can be:

> 9:00: Soils test being done in kitchen instead of office today as Barbara (9F) is home sick from school. Barbara is doing schoolwork while lying on living room sofa; her mother Martha is working on tests at the kitchen table. M: "When you get done with that page, Barbara, let me know and I'll take a look at it." B: "OK" M: "Soils tests are my least favorite job! It's embarrassing how long they take." Barbara enters, "Mommy, will you look at these? I still have more to do." M: "Sure, just let me finish this. OK, how many did you do? Good." B: "Can I rest?" M: "That's a good idea." B: "Can I watch TV?" M: "No, let's wait on that. You go lie on the sofa." Barbara returns to living room. Martha resumes using calculator to check over arithmetic. (Door to office is open— someone is talking on telephone there.) Quiet. Calculator continues, figuring done on paper. M. is now checking over schoolwork (arithmetic) on calculator.

> 9:10: M. gets up, takes schoolwork into living room, discusses it with Barbara, shows mistakes and how to correct them, watches B. rework it. Laughs. "72! Barbara look what you've got there!" Goes over procedure again. Finishes talking (five minutes) and tucks Barbara in, "Water wouldn't hurt you today either." Goes to kitchen sink, pours water for Barbara, to refrigerator for juice to add to glass, brings to Barbara in living room. B. then gets up, goes into kitchen for a second drink to take pill. She and mother stand at sink trying to get pill out of container. B. asks why pills have crease in middle, Mother: "So they break in half so little children can take it." B. returns to sofa. M. goes into adjacent room to start dryer. "That's one thing I have to remember to do during the day because (husband) is bothered by the sound of it" (if it runs in the evening).

> 9:20: Sits at kitchen table to resume soils test work. Plots areas on map and fills in dimensions and figures from report sheet. Does calculations from guidebook. Quiet. Only sounds are from dryer and occasional use of photocopier in office.

Trivial though such a modest example may seem, the ability to care for a sick child in such a non-disruptive manner symbolizes a significant distinction between work-at-home and most working families. Kamerman's (1980) study concluded that "child care continues to be the central problem for all employed mothers" (p. 131), a problem intensified by aggravations such as the sick child. Kamerman's conclusion that the work place provides no responsiveness or adaptation to parenting needs stands in contrast to a home work environment which can indeed bend where necessary to accommodate those needs.

Other observations further developed the image of child care as a subject of accommodation rather than a source of stress. The knitter who welcomed numerous visits from her children and grandchildren was observed once while a daughter-in-law and grandson were present as she worked, and again just after another group of grandchildren had completed a visit:

> 1:45: Asks husband to make a new pot of coffee. Finishes stitching and goes on to next sweater, piles that in box. "This week I had the kids (grandchildren). They're awfully good kids." Lays threads aside and starts stitching. Continues to talk about grandchildren while stitching.

Further evidence of the elasticity rather than inflexibility of child care was provided by two observations of the Martin family. The first occurred just prior to unanticipated open heart surgery for their preschool child, the second several weeks thereafter. The first observation showed the mother (a seamstress) working additional time to allow the family to stay in Portland during hospitalization. This observation included conversation preparing the daughter for her upcoming surgery:

> 8:50: Checks off on master list as each pattern is done. "Guess I need more green" (fabric. As she leaves she pauses to look at Darcy's (4F) picture and say. "That's nice!" Fetches fabric, returns to table, talks to daughter about impending heart surgery while cutting out pattern, "Tell Betty about the hospital," "What's the name of that special test?" etc.

And later in the same observation:

> Mother continues working, discusses readjustments for work around Darcy's hospitalization—projects worked on

ahead, plans for a friend to take over temporarily, orders ahead, etc.

The second observation occurred six weeks later and was marked by the recovering child dancing around, showing her scar, and her mother's comments on her good health.

Of the thirty observations, ten displayed behaviors relating to child care adaptability beyond the usual routine of children present during the day. While these examples of adaptability were not always profound, taken together they present convincing evidence of accommodation rather than conflict between work and family needs. Child care and related issues present, for most working parents, the greatest frustration and a principal source of disquiet about working. The lack of adequate high quality day care is a commonly acknowledged scandal and certainly a major impediment to women attempting to enter the male-structured workplace. Secondary day care issues, such as care for sick children not usually welcomed in day care facilities, adds a further burden. From simply the child care perspective, home work offers relief to overburdened parents. Potentially, it offers parents the opportunity to care for their own children while working, avoiding the often unrewarding search for good day care, and further permits the parent to bend flexibly in response to special child care needs, whether attending the school pageant or caring for the sick child.

Work-family accommodation also emerged in other observations, enhancing the sense of a dynamic rather than constrained or static relationship. "Family" is a key word in examining these adaptations because rarely was the worker responding as an individual; while a changed circumstance or event may have initiated with the worker, the family usually responded as well. Perhaps because these situations were fluid or short-lived, they were rarely mentioned in interviews; again, observations provided insight into such dynamics.

One such example is offered by a knitter's family. In the second observation, she mentioned that she planned to take a three-week, time intensive course which would necessitate rearrangements of work and family schedules:

They (husband and wife) talk about readjusting work when
Janet takes a three-week intensive course: picking up the

pace beforehand, John doing more of her knitting work, taking Alice (3F) off for the day, etc. Janet: "I can stand on my head for 2 weeks if I have to."

A second observation for the Dean family occurred subsequent to Mrs. Dean's acquisition of a second part-time job as a cashier in addition to her knitting duties. She had chosen a Thursday morning as a good time for me to observe her knitting but:

> 9:00: Arrival. Mrs. Dean in kitchen on phone searching for a babysitter. Store wants her to come in early today and she is trying to accommodate. After two more calls, arrangements are made.

> 9:10: We go into the living room where machine is set up facing TV. (She knits for the ensuing hour).

> 10:05: Pause. She goes to use bathroom. Returns. Says she'll have to stop early today because she has to go into work unexpectedly.

In a veterinarian's family, their full-time assistant had left work after the interview occurred. It was in observations that the effect on the family of the change in work conditions became apparent. The wife, who had previously assisted part-time, took over full-time work, resulting in the children having to eliminate some of their extra-curricular activities. The children were also called upon to provide more assistance:

> Mary (wife) picks up the phone as it rings, makes appointment for a laydown, "Do you want to be with him? Do you want to take care of the body?" Charles returns to the office with a sample receipt, they discuss what to buy and how many (forms). They decide and Mary calls in order. Charles walks into waiting room, "Here comes the UPS man." He greets him, they chat, packages are left on the examining room floor (medications to unpack). I ask if they typically set aside paperwork time or make it fit in where they can. Charles replies the latter, especially as they're shorthanded. He says Jenny (9F) has taken over sterilizing syringes with uneven success. Mary makes two more phone calls as Charles unpacks boxes.

For this family, the expectation was that the work rearrangement would be temporary and a new employee hired.

For the restaurant family, the wife's trip to a conference in Washington D.C. (she is a driving force in a local housing organization) was enabled by rearrangements of work assignments, and some preplanning. Though physically absent, she maintained involvement in the business by phoning nightly as the restaurant was opening:

> 5:20: Lisa (12F) goes off to brush hair in hall. Peter (father) asks "Where's your brother?" Lisa: "I don't know. I haven't seen him since school." Then Lisa asks, "What's for supper?" Asks father to get down rice pot for her restaurant work). Cat comes in meowing for food. Peter (humorously) "Do you think I run a restaurant?" Phone rings, Peter answers as Lisa cuts lemon wedges, washes and inserts parsley as garnish. She picks over parsley carefully for best pieces, cuts off stems and fits into lemons. Peter is still talking on phone (to wife) as he stands stirring potatoes. Conversation is revolving now around waitress call list for that evening, plans for museum, accumulated messages.

> 5:32: Lisa finishes garnishes, clears off counter of garnish materials (Peter still on phone), Lisa washes off counter, opens container of broccoli, waits for further instructions. Goes over to stir potatoes. Father passes phone to her. Lisa stands in hall talking to mother on phone.

In all, seven out of thirty observations indicated some degree of special work-family adaptation out of the usual routine. These seven, coupled with the ten child care adaptations, combine to lend credence to the concept of ongoing rather than static accommodation between work and family demands. Commonly, other family members participated in these adaptations, spreading responsibility around rather than relying solely on the worker to adjust to a need or problem. Involving others in finding solutions lessened the sense of pressure on the individual worker. For these families, the structural constraints of work schedule and job requirements which commonly impede work-family relationships were more malleable. Undeniably, conventionally employed families also create their own responses to work demands (witness split shift scheduling to handle child care), but their room for maneuverability is more restricted. A sense of stress is obviously aggravated by continual little crises—the sick child, the loss of an employee, the wish to take a course or attend a conference. The homely examples cited, while not impressive on their own, provide some sense of what stress over child care, or stress over conflicted work and family demands includes; such incidents operationalize stress. The ability to cope with these small incidents which collectively intensify stress is an indication of work and family accommodation.

JOB SATISFACTION

Consistent with the male work model, measurement of job satisfaction has traditionally been confined to intraoccupational characteristics—specific aspects of the job that contribute to or detract from the worker's gratification. Despite some suggestions that family balancing contributes to work quality, work satisfaction is usually measured as an attribute of the job or, minimally, residing within the individual's psyche.

Women, however, appear to present a different case. Although it might seem ludicrous to link the male executive's work satisfaction with the day care arrangement for his children, such a linkage figures more substantially in examining women's work lives. In fact, the major exception to the prevailing research tradition in job satisfaction has been among women, where studies of maternal employment usually pair work satisfaction with family outcome effects. Rarely, however, are the specific characteristics of the mother's jobs or the particular linkages between family and work satisfaction explored. What we do know is that the two variables seem related for women in ways which they are not for men, or at least in ways which are as yet uninvestigated for men. A general sense of conflict between home and work duties seems to operate for women in lowering job satisfaction but again the explicit dynamics are not usually spelled out. By contrast, study of men's interplay between work and family roles is minute in quantity, with a few exceptions. If women are indeed integrators, then findings indicating linkage between satisfaction in work and family spheres makes some sense. However, it is also possible that, were some of the same attention turned to men, and diversity rather than singularity among workers emphasized, similar results could emerge. A cautionary backdrop to this entire issue of work satisfaction is provided by Feldberg and Glenn (1982) who argue that men's work satisfaction has historically and prejudicially been measured through the "job model" of work-specific characteristics only, while women's work participation has invariably been examined through the "gender model" inevitably linking work and family characteristics.

Thus, while studies point to an often conflicted relationship between work and family demands for women, exemplified by the crucible of time, of which there is never enough to go around, and a less explicit relationship for men, the specific mediating factors in the conflict are unclarified.

Families working at home may provide some insight into these mediating variables. Certainly their responses to questions about job satisfaction demand that this issue be viewed as a systemic rather than individual one, as enmeshed as this work style is with family lives. Their concern with work autonomy which allows them to respond to family needs, as already reported, is one indicator of this link. Family motivations in choosing to work at home may provide a buttress to work satisfaction, allowing reconciliation of conflicting demands which produce endemic strain for workers in conventional employment. Time, a key indicator of the clash between work and family needs (General Mills 1981) is somewhat ameliorated for this sample by their greater sense of control over work and time processes. Thus, some sources of strain detrimental to job satisfaction (and consequently mediating variables in the relationship) are eliminated at the outset.

Further revealing of the links between job satisfaction and family life was the content of the participants' response to the question: "Please describe one time when work and family duties were in conflict. How did you resolve this?" If such a conflict is a cause of lower job satisfaction (Andrisani 1978), then answers to this question can serve as an indicator to job satisfaction among the participants as well as clarify the nature of these conflicts.

Of the fifteen participants, one woman reported that conflicts were not likely: "I think the demands on us aren't as rigid as somebody who stitches shoes or something. And there is usually some give there and we are pretty flexible." "Flexibility" and "lack of rigid demands" are probably not words routinely applicable to most work settings, settings in which conflict may indeed be inherent. The remaining fourteen participants reported conflicts (sometimes under prodding) that were occasional rather than endemic, limited rather than cataclysmic in nature, and invariably resolved in favor of family responsibilities through negotiation or sharing of duties. Of worthwhile note is that men in this study were as likely to resolve conflict in favor of family as were women, indicating either that they are quite dissimilar from most working men, or that they have freer rein to acknowledge family interests. Cited conflicts and resolutions include the following:

> W: It seems as though the only time that it would conflict, as far as this job's concerned, is let's say I had plans for this weekend and I got a call from the boss Friday night that she needed five sweaters rushed out Monday morning. I'd have to say, Sorry, I cannot make it. That way it would conflict. Or else I would do the rush work, if I wasn't going anywhere.

And:

> H: Well, like last Christmas, Christmas eve.
>
> I: Oh, No!
>
> H: I had sold a bunch of tires for Christmas presents. Well, of course, Christmas eve we always go to my folks' house and have their tree—a dinner and whatnot—a family get-together. Well, I sold a bunch of tires, so I was out there mounting up all of these tires, getting these people ready to go and in the meanwhile, I never had such a busy day.
>
> I: Christmas eve day?
>
> H: Everybody was coming in for tires, or to have tires fixed. And finally, I just had to lock the door and say, Hey, listen, I've got to be at my parents' house. Come back tomorrow— Christmas Day, I says, but I can't help you right now, I've got to go. And everybody was up there waiting for me (at parents').
>
> W: He was the only one not there.

H: And, you know, I felt bad, but I just had to tell them that I just had to leave. Ma and Dad, they're not getting any younger and whatnot, so I said, Well, I can't do that, you know, they always look forward to having all of us kids home Christmas eve. Christmas is a very special time, you know, for the old folks as well as the young folks and I just had to draw the line there and just tell the people that I had to go.

A woodworker's family experienced conflict this way:

I: You used to go on exhibit at shows—and you'd pack up the whole family.

W: Eight weeks in the summer and you know there are only eight weekends in the summer. Anyway, you'd go to these beautiful places and be on the wrong side of the booth. You know, we did that for two summers.

I: This was pre-son?

W: No.

I: Really?

W: In fact, this whole thing was post-son. He was fairly portable, especially the first summer. He didn't walk so he always stayed in one place when we did a show. The second year when he was hoofing it—he was into pulling down people's displays. And you know, shows are really tedious and everybody tells you how nice everything is and it gets old real quick.

I: Was that a mutual decision to give it up or did it just evolve that you decided you didn't need to do that?

H: No, we just decided there wasn't enough return.

I: So it wasn't a conflict in the sense that you were desperate to keep doing it?

W: No, right, I guess it wasn't. That was conflict in the family versus business, you know. We were using up the only weekends in the summer on these stupid shows. That was the extent of it. It was as much for our own mental health as a family or whatever.

Other reports of conflict were more mundane—attendance at a school pageant, too busy to cook supper, getting up in the morning in time for day care children's arrival—the common thread being that work duties received second place when a choice was inevitable, or that family members pitched in to help with necessary chores or work. Typical of these more routine responses was the following:

> W: Tuesday was my big workday instead of Monday. There is a children's dance class Tuesday afternoon and, once in a while somebody will come in and they'll stay half the morning and I can't kick them out. They don't come in often enough—if they did it that often I would, but I just can't and it would get so that I'd have to leave two sweaters unfinished or not go to dance class. So I'd go to dance class.

And:

> H: Yeah, I went away overnight last week and it was terrible. I hadn't done it alone in a long time. I went to Connecticut for two days. I had to go down for two reasons. When I finally got where I was going for my Thursday morning appointment, I called the guy up and asked him if he would meet me at his gallery Wednesday evening so that I could get up early on Thursday morning and drive home and be home in time for supper. And I was making good time on the way home, so I stopped in Massachusetts to look at some paintings that are going to be in this auction this week. Had I been running a little late, and if it was a choice between seeing the paintings a week early and missing supper with my family, I would have said, The heck with it, and I would have waited until the next week to see the paintings.

Claims of family priorities were given substantiation in several observations, though of course such instances of conflict were only seen through coincidence. In her interview, a hairdresser maintained that she controls her schedule, especially on Fridays, so that she is free on Friday afternoons to pick up a stepdaughter to spend the weekend. An observation two and one-half months later showed the following vignette:

> (Customer in chair getting hair cut). Conversation with customer results, her (customer's) sons like her to play basketball at the end of the day, "just what you want to do at the end of the day in the shop!" Customer asks for appointment for her son next Friday at 3:45. Hairdresser: "That's the time I usually get Diane" (her stepdaughter), though that's also

the son's best time to come for a haircut. They ultimately find another date.

In another observation of a fine art dealer who claimed he wanted to evolve a more home and family centered workstyle, time spent on work occupied twenty minutes of the two-hour period; the remaining time was spent playing with children and doing yard work. His casual workstyle reflected accurately his comments delivered in interview about his work habits receiving second place to his family life.

A second, more direct measure of work satisfaction was taken by the question, "If there were a comparable job available to you right now in a more conventional setting, would you accept it?" Eleven responses were firmly negative, couched in terms of pleasure with the flexibility of the job and personal happiness. Four participants gave conditional answers, appreciating the economic security that would be available in a conventional job but wondering whether the trade-off in autonomy would be worth it. The essence of their answer was that a job change would depend on the specific circumstances of the job. (None of the participants changed jobs during the six months of data gathering).

For these workers, then, job satisfaction is indeed partially rooted in intraoccupational conditions. However, the whole picture of satisfaction is complete only when the link to family interaction is made; that is, fairly autonomous circumstances on the job allow these individuals to perceive less stress and more accommodation between work and family, to draw upon family assistance when necessary to find resolution, and to make comfortable elections of family priorities when choice is required.

FAMILY IDEOLOGY

Determining whether values influence a family's behavior or the reverse is true is beyond the scope of this study. Indeed, family ideology has not been a notable research field in family studies other than through inference. The imprecise link between belief and practice does not lend itself easily to interpretation. Nonetheless, several results emerging from this study suggest that it is important to consider how families perceive themselves and how they link that perception to practice. First, there is an unequivocal interplay among work, parent, spouse, and child roles in these families, concretizing the link between family and work worlds and guaranteeing that values will be mutually infusing rather than characteristically isolating. The instances of whole family involvement and support noted suggest some commonality of values and practice among family members. Second, the conscious choice of home work as an alternative, distinct work style indicates the deliberate exercise of some value system. Third, the internal focus of these participants on home, individual, and family-centered activities rather than external group-oriented activities suggests some preference for family values. Finally, specific examples such as parents wishing to be more available to their children, demonstrating this availability through interruptibility, and children's consequent verbalized appreciation of parental availability connotes a mutually shared value system. Perhaps more than the average worker, these families actively join values and practice in linking work and family lives. The special circumstances of working at home permit family and worker to explore more fully where these linkages lie. Conventional workplace barriers typically demand that the worker dichotomize work and family values and practice, virtually ensuring conflict rather than reconciliation between beliefs and behaviors suitable for one system and not the other. By contrast, in home-working families, the integration of space and time creates a scenario for integrating values and practice as well.

To elicit thoughts about value and practice, one interview question asked: "When you think of what a family should be like, how does this type of work arrangement fit in?" Some workers expressed the link between value and practice succinctly and clearly:

> I feel good about my family. If I went out to work, I wouldn't, and if I didn't do anything at all I wouldn't.

And:

> I don't make my family fit my work—I make my work fit my family.

And:

Makes the family closer. With what's going on, like she said, our daughter (9F) says it's time to go to work so she helps with (her little sister) and everybody pitches in. . . .

And:

Well, as far as the ideal family, I don't think there is any such thing as an ideal family. But I do believe, I'm hoping that it will fit in because I'd like to have my boys, you know, be independent and be in the business industry and I feel that by doing that I'm giving them responsibility that they ordinarily wouldn't have.

I: That's true.

H: And I definitely want them to grow up, you know, being responsible.

I: Okay. That's a good example.

W: Another way, ah, with the boys out there, they meet the public and they also learn how to be respectable (sic) to other people. You know, instead of mouthing off at them, they know how to be respectable toward them and respect them.

Other responses were more philosophical:

(The wife of one home worker):

W: It's my philosophy. Men have been taken out of parent-ing—I don't know if it happened with the industrial revolu-tion or if it's just that women are smarter, but anyway that's a place where Charles is involved with them. I think it teaches them responsibility—someplace where he has to put up with the mess and deal with it, and they have to learn that he's human.

And:

H: I think this is as close as it gets. I think I try hard at it—at the "Little House on the Prairie" family, you know, or whatever. I try really hard.

And:

W: I think being here we've had opportunities with the girls that we wouldn't have had if we'd been working out. We've been here when they need us. I know I like to have Barry here at noontime. I mean, it's nice to have him home at noon. You don't have to try and remember if, you know, things have happened through the whole day; you can talk about them right then. I just think that we've had a lot more time together because of our being here than we would have had otherwise.

Similar sentiments were voiced by other participants, inevitably joining the chosen work style to a family arrangement which they found satisfying. Prizing family life, they recognized the benefits that an out-of-the-mainstream work style afforded them. Further, their valuing of family life received validation in practice, with frequent tangible instances of family priorities and needs being met. Rather than discontinuity between work-values and family-values, there was consonance. Instead of inhabiting segregated spheres with dichotomous values, there was a more seamless integration of values. Remarkable here is the worker's opportunity to live out values, to adjust work and family lives to a satisfactory personal balance, to control the practice of these values, and to count upon the support of family members in sustaining and carrying out these values. For workers who share these values but who function in the conventional work world, such opportunities are rare.

GENDER ROLE

A second aspect of family ideology that emerged during the study concerned gender role. Although no interview question directly addressed the issue, general comments and observations developed some sense of the beliefs and practices revolving around men's and women's roles in these homes. Avowedly family-centered as these families claimed to be, one might anticipate an extremely conservative family role constellation. This proved not to be predictably the case, however, as a far more complex picture emerged. As noted earlier, home workers reported substantial spousal participation in household chores (thirteen out of fifteen) and child care (all fifteen). Researchers in the area of gender role might find such reports surprisingly contradictory to most data indicating only creeping increments in men's household work, though more notable increases in child care. Most studies of gender role and family life focus narrowly on who does what tasks and how much time such tasks require, both readily quantifiable measures. Unfortunately, such a restricted approach ignores many of the more interesting negotiations that occur among couples grappling with major change in their lives. Lein (1982) cautions importantly that this restricted approach disregards the role that perception plays. Since we have already seen numerous instances of perception's significance in affecting work and family interaction among these families, her caution deserves emphasis:

> There is a tacit assumption in much discussion of housework that allocation of tasks is a direct reflection of the degree to which a family believes in an egalitarian or sex-segregated model of family life. In fact, attitudes toward housework and the allocation of tasks do not have such a straightforward relationship to family ideology. (Lein 1982, 2)

From this point of view, the precise balance of household and child care chores may not be as significant as the individual's perception of that balance. Thus, the knitter who acknowledged her logger-husband's expanded family role and decreased work role during spring break-up (and her consequent decreased family role and increased work role) may rightly see her husband as fulfilling a large share of household and child care duties:

> W: During spring break-up (ice-out and mud-season) when he is not working very much, he takes over the housework. He is real good with the kids. Anytime that he is home, if the weather is bad or on Saturday, if he goes to Bangor for parts or something, he'll pile 'em right in and he'll take 'em all, and boy is that a hard job—the three of 'em.
>
> I: That's to be admired!
>
> W: I don't even attempt that. When I get my groceries, they each have a turn every week, they alternate and I take one with me. Taking three and going into a store is really hard because they all go in different directions. Last week with that storm he (husband) was home all day, and the other day he was home at three o'clock, and he got supper and he did the dishes and, you know, he helps a lot that way.

I: On a day like that when he was around, would you knit longer or knit more?

W: Yah, I knit longer, you know, and then I was done earlier, I didn't knit from 8:00 to 10:00 p.m.

I: Okay. Oh, that's interesting—so if he's home to help with your daughter or the housework, that frees you up to just get your (knitting) work done.

W: And when he's not working in the spring, I will work more. I'll try to put in forty hours a week or even more than that because we'll miss the money. He will be working some, but a lot less.

While helping with housework may be a red flag to egalitarians, indicating that such labor is still within the female province, this is not this woman's perception, who sees her views changing. In fact, earlier she says: "The older I get, the more of a liberated person I am; because I wasn't when I was younger at all."

She then goes on to describe her children's involvement in household work, insisting that both girls and boy participate in all chores from firewood stacking to cleaning, "so there was no need of him not doing the things that most people would think just the girls ought to be doing."

Most other home workers expressed similar sentiments. One knitter recounted how she insisted that all her sons learn to knit:

Even my boys, if I was sitting there knitting when they were tiny, they learned the work. And they all knit. In fact, this one—up in Caribou—has made three quilts. He knits. They've got one baby and he knit his mittens and hat. A family that doesn't co-operate—if a man figures that she has her place and he has his place, she does her work and he does his work—that wouldn't fit there at all.

For some men, having a home-working wife forced them to take up additional household responsibilities, acknowledging that her involvement in paid labor right in front of their eyes made it difficult to ignore the unequal burden she was carrying; several conceded that her income met or exceeded theirs and thus fairness demanded their increased participation in other chores.

The reverse of the sharing (admittedly not necessarily equal) of housework and child care is reflected in the assistance which home workers reported was provided by their spouse in fulfilling work duties, as previously reported. This creates a sense of flux in roles between partners, both fulfilling household, child care, and home work functions though in varying degrees. No family portrayed itself as avowedly egalitarian with clearly apportioned household responsibilities; five families described themselves as fairly traditional in division of labor. The bulk of the families approximate what Lein (1982) characterizes as the "Helping Out" Model:

> Housework remains the woman's responsibility and her primary function, but both husbands and wives agree that because of the time and energy consumed by her paid work and the importance of the wife's paid work to the family, she requires as much help as possible from her husband in maintaining the home. Therefore, just as the wife's contributions to the family income are perceived to be genuine and important, so the husband's contributions to the home are perceived as necessary and a significant help to her in fulfilling family responsibilities. (Lein 1982, 17)

Lein maintains that this model requires frequent, ongoing negotiation about household work, and thus captures the state of flux which many families report around issues of spouse involvement in work. One example of the fallout of this ongoing negotiation is captured in the following excerpt from a knitter's husband. He had previously worked in a mill but her increased knitting income enabled him to quit millwork and stay at home as a househusband in a major role change. Now that his wife no longer performed the bulk of the household chores, he gained insight into what housework really meant:

> H: Women have always had that tradition—they've been brought up having a thousand and one little jobs to do around the house every day. And sometimes you can't fulfill them all, or you can't even fulfill one individual one, but you have to attack each problem as it comes up. There is breakfast, there is dinner, there is lunch or whatever, and each of them has to be taken care of, whereas a man is used to leaving home, going to work, punching the card—he does four

hours right there at a very specific time—then he has his lunch and he punches that card again and works another four hours. It's great because the woman has a completely different attitude. The time is very fluid for a woman. It's like the tide going in and out, whereas for a man it's like a drawbridge coming down and going up.

Chapter 8

Construing Integration

Women pull things together rather than break
them apart: they don't set off their careers from
their families; they try to mold both into a whole,
to stretch themselves to encompass both without
detracting from either. (Klagsbrun 1985, 137)

And I think the people who are out in the work-
a-day world can't possibly work at effectively
reaching the other goals—you know, the other
parts of their life—but I think this is as close as
I can get (home-working father).

Molding both career and family into a whole and reaching
the other parts of life express the challenge of reconnect-
ing work and family lives. Families seeking balance struggle
against an array of individualistic work world values which
neither invite nor support family concerns; at most, employers offer a limited range of options (such as flextime or parental leave) which only minimally and temporarily interrupt
customary work world practices. Seeking alternatives, some
observers favor a more harmonious relationship which infuses family values of collectivity, care for other, and intrinsic
reward into the workplace. Such a vision is shared by feminists like Gilligan (1982) and futurists such as Toffler (1980)
who see positive benefits accruing to family and society by re-
aligning male and female worlds. However, "visionary" best
characterizes this goal, one as yet untranslated into workplace practice.

What, then, can working families do, barring any meaningful employer practices supporting reconciliation? Principally, they fall back upon themselves, piecing together whatever eclectic patchwork of alternatives best suits their needs and resources. Consistent with historical tradition, families still create their own strategies where possible. For example, Lein (1974) identified split-shift scheduling, where parents deliberately work different shifts in order to avoid putting their children in day care settings. In this way, both parents work and both parents provide child care, albeit in a sequential rather than simultaneous partnership. A more recent study underscores the continuing importance of split-shift scheduling as a contemporary work-family strategy. Focusing on a national sample of young, dual-earner parents of preschool children, Presser (1988) discovered that nearly one-third of such mothers and fathers worked different shifts. These families relied heavily on spousal care as a child care arrangement, indicating that sequential parental care represents an alternative chosen by many families.

A similar creative response comes from female entrepreneurs who represent one of the fastest-growing employment categories of the past decade. Recognizing the lack of employment alternatives consonant with caring for children, increasing numbers of women have turned to self-employment, initiating small-scale ventures (often located in their homes) as a preferred outlet. Women choosing this alternative—home-based self-employment—represent more than half of all full time home-working women (Horvath 1986). Part-time work, too, maintains its status as a desirable work option among married women. In general, married women with young children continue to choose or create alternative work strategies where possible, persisting in a search for greater responsivity.

Home work represents one of these potential options. In common with other strategies, it has drawbacks. On a cultural and political level, the need for women to create alternative arrangements exemplifies their continued inequality in the workplace. Home work particularly has been condemned as a symbol of that inequality, depicting so graphically women's continued assumption of both work and family burdens (Boris 1987).

Living in the imperfect society we inhabit, such critiques merit discussion. Debates over home work reflect much broader, justifiable concerns about gender and political inequality, and asymmetrical family responsibilities. Nonetheless, this study's intent has been to refocus on the family system itself rather than deal with broader concerns which others are addressing. Because integration of work and family life may express itself in varied forms, it is critical to pause and examine those forms before proceeding to larger debates. As these forms emerge naturally, without imposed or dictated patterns, they provide important clues about the quality of the future relationship between work and family. Thus far, polemic has often preceded careful inquiry into these emerging forms, and "molding into a whole" and "reaching the other parts of your life" more frequently express longings or theoretical positions than specific designs. Essentially, these new definitions are being assembled and lived out by individual families rather than by social prescription. Quietly, these families are redefining the interaction of two powerful social systems as they filter the experience of each through their own perceptions. On one level, this redefinition is very personal, pragmatic, bound within the intimate web of the family's life. This elemental level of integration responds to very practical concerns immediate to the family itself: what's important for us? How do I spend more time with my children? How do I nurture and earn income—are they incompatible? What work structures can we adopt to allow us to work and love simultaneously? What happens daily, concretely, when we try to do this? It is this elemental level of pragmatism which usually motivates people to search out alternatives rather than more idealistic visions.

Home-working families, as we have seen, are principally inspired by these very personal, pragmatic motivations. Indeed, over the past few chapters, we have spent a great deal of time examining relatively minute features of their daily lives. Several reasons justify such attention to detail. One is that we know very little about the daily lives of working families and how they handle the interaction of work and family. Simply as a set of data, such details provide useful empirical information. Second, examining families' lives removes us from polemic and draws us closer to human reality, helping us to understand more accurately and sympathetically what reconciling and balancing imply. Much of the public writing on home work stakes out ideological positions, often reflecting the historical view of home work as an exploitive menace ("Home Industry Evil Is Back," Porter 1983). Other views express favorable sentiment while neglecting actual details ("Home Computers Are Nurturing Working Mothers," Faries 1983). Polemic from whatever viewpoint often makes assumptions about family's lives which are not grounded in reality, blinding us to immediate and personal consequences for families. Devoting some attention to those actual details corrects this oversight.

Third, the tangibility of families' work alternatives illustrates keenly the creativity and versatility with which families respond to external demands. Most American families must work to survive economically, but the way in which they execute this work is far from uniform. Large scale statistical data obscures this variety and versatility, an expression of family strength. Taking the time to examine carefully and patiently individual families' responses rights this imbalance and increases our respect for their functioning. This is not to say that families are marvelously autonomous and completely healthy but it does redress the view that they are merely pawns of larger social forces.

Finally, by focusing on families' lives, we perceive with greater clarity their definitions of integration. We can see more tangibly how they translate integration from vague goal to feasible daily reality. This translation also reveals in its minutiae a subversive threat to the larger work world. Interestingly, it is the pedestrian details of these families' lives that most dramatically challenge the prevailing work world's values. Choosing to be available to children, setting work aside to respond to spouse and children, groping toward more gender role sharing, saying no to work demands, and flexibly controlling work time and space collectively challenge work's primacy in our lives. Such activities assail and weaken work's position as the prime criterion of twentieth-century man's identity. Work's stranglehold on the daily structure and routine of our lives—our ascribed place in a hierarchy, our expectations of the life span, our relationship with children, our standards of masculinity and femininity—is loosened by such simple daily examples as the woman who puts her work aside to read to her children, or the man who takes his family to the beach for the day instead of working.

Ironically, then, these families' homeliness illustrates profoundly the clash of work world-family world values, a clash some conceptualize as a gender conflict as well. Integrating work and family life, then, is a deceptive process. At one level, it is simply a personal effort to readjust work and family demands, an individual or family's attempt to become more responsive to family needs. However, this readjustment also marks the inherent tension between two major value systems and the far-reaching consequences flowing from that conflict. Neutral or even positive terms such as integrating, balancing, reconciling, or fusing mask this underlying struggle.

This chapter follows the route of those consequences from the family's point of view. First, we'll review some of the specific conditions relevant to families in this study, suggesting factors which support and hamper the use of home work among them. The second part of the chapter discusses the context affecting those conditions, linking findings in this study with those of other home-working families.

RECAPITULATING THE HOME WORK STRATEGY: THE FAMILY'S VIEW

Reviewing the experiences of families in this study reminds us that integration can exist, that it can express itself in a specific form, and that this particular expression may not be an appropriate choice for all families. Rather, home work exists as one choice along a continuum of work-family integration; a desirable choice for some families, other families might be better served by choosing elsewhere along that continuum.

Families participating in this study perceived themselves as satisfied with a work style which allowed them to integrate work and family processes quite concretely. It would be unrealistic to assume that what works for them would be a prescription for other families seeking the same balance. Clearly, individual motivations and characteristics as well as family support played a major role in sustaining such a work style, key factors which not every potential home worker could rely on. How could a worker and his/her family determine that this might present a desirable strategy? Findings from these families suggest that the individual who values workplace socialization, prizes job status and recognition, identifies primarily with his or her role as a worker, and cannot tolerate interruption or disorganization to the work process would be unhappy in such a setting. Further, it appears that a successful home worker must value autonomy highly, perhaps even holding some negative feelings about conventional work experiences, in order to bolster the appeal of home work. Spouses and children who participate in and support this work choice make success more likely. The inevitable drawing together of work and family roles might appeal to spouses working in concert but not to those preferring distance between these arenas. These are some of the personal and family characteristics that might operate positively for some individuals considering home work and negatively for others.

Other possible detrimental factors emerge as well. Economic insecurity, mentioned by participants as the chief disadvantage of home work, presents a significant obstacle to families accustomed to regular paychecks. Other negatives of home work mentioned by participants included lack of fringe benefits and occasional feelings of isolation. Obviously, participants in this study perceived the positives as outweighing the negatives. A study of disgruntled or former home workers would reveal more negatives.

Although unmentioned by the participants, other potential drawbacks emerge. For many families, too much family togetherness would be a negative. Excessive sharing of roles, space, time and interests may prevent healthy individual development. Individuals valuing their privacy and distinct sense of self, plus leisure activities apart from the family, might find home work quite unsuitable. Home work does not necessarily provide a setting for family pathology, however; whether it results in pathology or positive family life very much depends on how the individual worker and family mediate the situation—again, their phenomenology.

Although no instances of exploitation or abuse were observed or reported in these successfully working families, the potential for such exploitation exists. The difficulty of observing, regulating, and protecting work conditions in the privacy of the home (and indeed whether the home should be invaded for purposes of regulation) lies at the heart of the contemporary debate over home work prohibitions. Children in such a situation could be especially vulnerable to labor exploitation or abuse by an overworked parent. However, it needs reemphasis that children interviewed and observed for this study felt very positively about the accessibility of their parents' work. Such benefits to children should not be forgotten in concern about possible exploitation. Conceivably the child of a conventionally employed parent who sees that parent for only one-half hour a day between babysitter and bedtime may be more endangered.

Although participants in this study represented a diversity of occupations, the size of the group was inadequate to draw conclusions relating the nature of the individual occupation to family life. For example, the one participant with the most intellectually demanding job (translator), presumably allowing the least amount of interruption, had a child in grade school and consequently adapted her work schedule to that of the school day. Had that child been a preschooler, the conflict of combining an intellectual job with child care might have been more apparent. An individual with an occupation demanding uninterrupted time might find the intermixing of work and family life more onerous. Further studies of home workers in varying occupational categories will illuminate the relationship of the nature of work and work-family integration more adequately.

Also not to be overlooked is the value of a supporting culture for those who choose to work at home. A rural area traditionally valuing family life, lack of alternative employment opportunities in a low-income area, the existence of a low-consumption culture which does not emphasize material goods, a widely distributed rural population without public transportation to deliver workers to central workplaces, the absence of government prohibitions on home work (notably local zoning controls), low crime rates which free the home workers of concern about personal danger, all combine to support a home work life style. In the absence of such a supporting culture, undertaking home work might be exceptionally difficult and unrewarding. Again, the context of the situation cannot be ignored.

All these potentially limiting and/or negative features of home work exist. Home work's success or failure as a family strategy depends heavily on intrafamily dynamics. For the individual family interested in constructing its own model of integration through a home work strategy, several critical features emerged among the study's families. These features unify and rationalize this choice in the following ways.

1. *The Importance of Perceived Meaning.* Crucial to the success of this work style for these families is their perception that they have achieved a satisfactory integration of work and family life. The critical significance of their own perception of the situation cannot be overlooked for it transforms working conditions that for some people would be intolerable (isolation, interruption, relative economic insecurity) into virtues. Choosing this work style in preference to others, perceiving oneself as having control over work and time processes, wishing to be available to one's children, feeling capable of responding to emergencies or changes in routine—all are important expressions about the relationship of work and family. Indications that some systemic family phenomenology may operate (for example, parents wishing to be available to children and children appreciating and taking advantage of that availability) only buttress the significance of perceptions in evaluating the home work experience.

Social scientists have traditionally ignored questions of perceptions about work in favor of more objective analyses, but findings here emphasize the limitations of that approach. Renshaw (1976), one of the few researchers to consider phenomenology as a key variable in work-family investigation, found that an individual's "perceived influence" (not actual or objective power) was critical to handling work-family stress, an outcome consistent with this study's findings. Rapoport and Rapoport (1976) also attended to their participants' own perceptions of dual career issues, but generally such a focus is missing from the literature. Clearly, such a phenomenological concern is what Bronfenbrenner and Crouter (1982) suggest would enrich the future direction of work-family study, admitting that it will require new paradigms not currently appreciated in mainstream social science.

A consideration of phenomenology also provides a significant link with historical research which has highlighted the importance of family strategy regarding work choices. The concept that families, especially women, made deliberate decisions to adjust work arrangements to meet varying family needs has been amply demonstrated. Family strategy, rooted as it is in assessing family, individual, and economic needs and then constructing the most appropriate solution, represents phenomenology in historical perspective. Although lacking the opportunity to interview long-dead subjects to determine their perceptions, historical researchers have made good use of existing data sources to develop the concept of family strategy. Social science, with readier access to live subjects, has been somewhat less inclined to embrace it. In this particular light, work-at-home families provide possibilities for both fields: the perceptions of families in this study corroborate the existence of family strategy. The specific aspects of that phenomenology—how and why they make the decisions they do about work—offer social science directions for research.

2. *Space and Time Access as Enablers.* The most concrete demonstration of work and family interaction occurred in space and time access. More than mere tools of analysis, space and time assumed identity and significance of their own as facilitators of integration. The ready access of family members to workspace and the interruptibility of work time characteristic of these families resulted in perceived positive consequences for family life. Workers saw themselves in control of their work schedule and thus able to respond to family needs without undue difficulty; children were able to see their parents at work and to participate in that work in ways which were natural and developmentally appropriate; spouses both assisted in that work and recognized benefits to themselves of that work style. The lack of rigid space and time boundaries underlay many of these perceived positive consequences. Whether such dramatic interplay of work and family activities could have occurred in a more structured and less permeable space and time context is open to question. Clearly, such ready access supported families' perceptions of holding work and family demands in greater balance.

Families' utilization of space and time in this study also amplified research use of those terms. Most research, as previously noted, has examined time solely in terms of its allocability to either work or family. In this study, allocation was not the major issue. A far more crucial component of time was its flexibility—how it could be punctuated, reconstructed and made malleable to respond to family needs. Observations, interviews, and logs repeatedly stressed the non-uniformity of time and therefore its consequent value. Contrary to most previous research use of time as a tool of analysis, work time for these families was not apportionable, invariable or predictable. Even more salient, these families dramatically extended the concept of time beyond narrow considerations of length of workday typically employed by researchers. For these families, several elements of time emerged: the daily work time, which varied considerably both for the individual and within the group; yearly fluctuations in time, either resulting from seasonal changes (the knitter whose pulp truck driver husband lost work during spring break-up) or from responsibility to individual variations (the sick child); and finally the possibility of life cycle time, particularly suggested by the number of women with preschool children who chose to work at home. The most striking summary of these families' use of time lies in its unpredictability and responsivity. By contrast, work time studies which focus on conventional work schedules appear anemic.

For time to be as malleable as it proved to be for these families, however, space access was a necessary precondition. Work literature generally ignores space issues, the assumption being that work space and family space are separate and inaccessible to one another. Although a few studies have tentatively suggested the positive benefits to families of permeable work boundaries (Piotrkowski 1978), little meaningful investigation of workspace access vis-a-vis family boundaries has taken place. Evidence from home-working families strongly reinforces that space merits far greater consideration as a variable in work-family adjustment than it has thus far received. Although not every family can have home-workplace combinations, certainly there are varying degrees of family access to conventional workplaces: the small business where children drop by to say hello to a parent after school, the on-site day care, the large corporation that prohibits family visits, the after school phone calls to working parents from children. Trimberger and MacLean (1982) suggested that familiarity with parental work facilitates a child's adjustment to maternal employment. Building on that finding, a simple study correlating workspace accessibility and child adjustment to parental employment offers considerable potential. Evidence from work-at-home families suggests the value of extending the space access issue in other directions as well: spousal knowledge and involvement in work resulting from degree of access, employer policies encouraging family access as related to employee satisfaction, and family-work stress as related to workspace access, among others.

More significantly, shared space influences families in a far more potent and subtle way. Workspace access and the physical work-family interaction it promotes is both important and tangible. Perhaps more meaningful, however, is shared space's effect on gender role within the household. Home working families' experience suggests that sharing work and family space encourages more sharing of work and family roles. Although little overt investigation of such a possibility has occurred, some historians have suggested that shared work and family space in pre-industrial time may have meant that sex roles were less rigidly prescribed (Cott 1977). Vanek's (1980) study of farm families found that shared space and its consequent integration of work, family, and leisure roles promoted gender equality rather than segregation. The Rapoports (1976, 97–150) reported on one dual-career family which worked at home, more thoroughly "interpenetrating" work and family worlds than any other couple. Their family pattern was characterized by marked flexibility in fulfilling work and family roles and the children being " 'mixed up in' the lives of their parents to an extent you'd hardly believe" (Rapoport and Rapoport 1976, 131). Similarly, Golden's (1975) intensive study found that one family with "diffuse" boundaries between work and family life was characterized by greater interdependence and family togetherness. Surely such findings emphasize the subtlety with which space access influences family interaction, though the exact mechanics remain unclear. Kanter (1977, 14) suggests that physically separate workplaces afforded men a "retreat from intimacy" which allowed them to remain aloof from family involvement. The reverse of that situation seems to indicate that non-separate workplaces promote family involvement. Considerable room remains for further research into space's subtle effects on work-family life.

These families' experiences, while hardly definitive, suggest that work siting might provide one significant key to unlocking the complex interplay of work, family, and gender role expectations. Lacking the protectively impermeable barrier of the normal workplace, it appears that work and family roles flow together in the home work site. Regardless of initial motivation for working at home, men and women develop some commonality between work and family duties, a sharing either sought (principally by women) or gradually developed (more typically by men). Obviously, the precise nature and degree of such sharing varies with the characteristics of the family involved but a home workspace appears to offer a nudge in that direction.

LINKS WITH OTHER   OME-WORKING FAMILIES

The previous section's focus on home work as an integrative strategy concentrated on some of the intrafamily dynamics encouraging its success. This final section speculates on the conditions supporting those intrafamily dynamics by relating them to characteristics found among other home-working families. This study's intensive scrutiny of the daily lives of home-working families distinguishes it from related research which more frequently emphasizes the home worker her/himself and employs different methods of investigation. Nonetheless, this developing body of research shares a concern with home work as a strategy and its role in family-work interaction. The experiences of fifteen rural Maine home-working families provide no basis for generalization in the conventional statistical sense, and I make no effort to imply that. Legitimately, however, their experiences present us with one fund of information, information which can be compared with other home-working families' experiences, or "transferred" rather than "generalized" (Guba 1981). By comparing, we can gradually build an inventory of key elements affecting home work outcomes. Thus, this section takes that final step of examining outcomes from this study and relating them to findings reported elsewhere. Throughout, the family itself remains the pivotal unit of analysis; again, no attempt is made to encompass broad social and political analysis.

Families in this study reported numerous positive effects of home work, a viewpoint contradicted by most researchers who take a more dour perspective (Boris 1987; Christensen 1985; Johnson 1982). Does their existence invalidate these Maine families' experiences? Kraut and Grambsch (1987) discuss these opposing stances, noting the "optimistic one based on case studies of home-based workers using computer technology and a pessimistic one rooted in labor history" (p. 411). The optimistic viewpoint cites employment flexibility afforded by home work while the negative one underscores the potential for exploitation. Which is correct?

Helpfully, Kraut and Grambsch's examination of census data for home-based white collar workers suggests areas of reconciliation. They found that certain groups are "differentially susceptible" to home work and concluded: "Different demographic groups differ in their familial obligations and resources and in their physical capabilities in ways that place constraints on the places and times they can work" (1987, 423). For some of these people, home work may indeed represent an attractive work strategy which offers needed flexibility. Among the groups found to be heavily involved in white collar home work were mothers, rural residents, the elderly, and the disabled.

Relating such findings to the present study suggests several mutual areas. Rural residence promotes home work for a number of reasons, most of them rooted in the distinctive nature of the rural economy. Unlike urban residents who may choose work options from a varied array, rural families lack such a degree of choice. Instead, "rural economies are generally simple, characterized by one or two major industries, either natural-resource based nondurable manufacturing, or tourism," a restricted range of work opportunities at the unskilled or semiskilled level further limited by "seasonal production and the economic cycles which these industries experience" (Teal 1981, 28). Traditional rural economies offer few attractive, upwardly mobile job opportunities. One study participant described this limited selection and the consequent appeal of home work very well:

If you were working in Detroit making $12-$15 an hour, you could make a good argument for going and doing it. But when you're making the kind of money a lot of people make around here and you're living quite literally hand-to-mouth, you never actually get one foot ahead of the other, you say to yourself: Well there is one thing I can do for myself. If there is some way I can make a few bucks and stay home at the same time, then hang up the factory job because you're not going to get ahead anyway. So you may as well stay home and not get ahead.

In response to such a limited job selection, rural families often patch together a diverse array of work options; in parts of rural Maine, occasional factory jobs supplemented by seasonal part-time work as blueberry pickers, woods workers, Christmas wreath makers and clam diggers are common examples. Thus, a familiar standard of work alternatives exists in rural areas, one which encourages rural residents to consider home work as a feasible choice.

Also contributing to rural residents' inclination to home-based work in a more positive vein is the presence of "micro-businesses":

> The economies of many rural areas are still made up of thousands of micro-businesses: cottage industries; one- or two-person service firms; low-volume and seasonal shops; labor-intensive manufacturing operations out of kitchens, barns, and sheds; small specialized mail-order outfits; artisans and crafters; and small-scale agriculture. (Teal 1981, 28)

The widespread presence and visibility of such microbusinesses, so familiar to rural residents, increase home work's acceptability as an honorable work alternative. Further, certain conservative values long attributed to rural residents, notably an emphasis on independence and a concern for family life, also rationalize home work's appeal. Families in this study certainly displayed attitudes and activities consistent with those values.

Other characteristics of rural residence mentioned in chapter 3, such as lack of zoning controls, also foster the acceptance of home work as a reasonable work option. Families in rural economic settings, then, quite likely experience home work in a more supportive manner than the non-English speaking illegal immigrant in an urban slum, for example.

From the family's point of view, it may indeed be perceived as a desirable choice.

Large scale survey data link these Maine families with other home-working families in additional ways. Consistently, family structure shows up as a key variable in describing home workers. Kraut and Grambsch's (1987) review disclosed that women in intact families with young children were over-represented in their sample of white collar home workers. Although families in this Maine study were not necessarily white collar, they share the characteristic of being two-parent households with children. Such households obviously have greater resources than a single-parent, female headed household, for example. For the two-parent, two-income household, home work may indeed offer a feasible work option: one (external) income provides a cushion of financial support for the home worker. Beyond the security of income, an outside job may also offer the fringe benefits of medical insurance less likely to accompany home work. With child care expenses usually representing the largest drain on family income after housing and food, a home-working parent may look even more attractive. Such circumstances represent the "differential susceptibility" to home work mentioned earlier. When two-parent rural households report satisfaction with home work, they may be accurately assessing their own needs and resources.

Popular literature frequently emphasizes the appeal of working at home for women with young children. Survey data underscores this rationale for home work, noting that women typically cite the presence of young children as the prime motivation for working at home (Christensen 1987). Certainly the Maine families in this study fit this picture. Further, they provide some sense of how child care and work might coexist, sketching in an understanding of a complex mutuality between parenting and working in such settings. Currently, although survey data indicate that many women attempt to combine working and parenting through home work, we have little knowledge of the mechanics of such interaction. Some researchers maintain that successful home-working women must rely on supplemental child care, or adapt work to school hours (Christensen 1987). Families in this study provide less a sense of "either-or" child care and more of a "back and forth" child care orientation. Importantly, they suggest that child care is not an isolated issue but rather a part of a fairly complex relationship between work and family life, one which encompasses parenting and working rather than dividing them. It seems likely that further investigation of home-working families in other circumstances will enlarge our appreciation of the diversity with which parenting and working fit together rather than isolating any single pattern.

These families' experiences also suggest the value of enlarging the scope of our examination beyond the mother-child dyad so often the center of attention in home-working families. Without denying children's significant role in impelling and sustaining this work arrangement, home work effects also spilled over into other aspects of family life, implicating spouses as well. For these families, the involvement of spouses and the perceived sense of family adaptiveness were key elements in a true work-family system. Thus, home work appears to be "absorptive," Kanter's (1977) term for occupations that extend beyond the worker him/herself to "implicate other family members and command their direct participation in the work system in either its formal or informal aspects" (p. 26). Regardless of the specific occupation, home work for families in this study appeared to be quite absorptive; recall one father's comment that "our family has become our business. I mean it's all so integrated that the other (separate identity) is impossible." Kanter maintained that a study of these absorptive, coextensive workplaces would prove fruitful for family researchers drawn to their unique effects on family behavior, relationships, and dilemmas. The tentative directions suggested by findings in this study support her prediction.

Findings in this and related studies also alert us that home work may be a life stage related arrangement. Throughout discussion of home work, we have underscored its link with family structure and dynamics. The connection between women, home work, and family should remind us that home work may lose its appeal once children grow older. Horvath's (1986) data showed that progressively fewer women worked at home as the ages of their children increased, with the lowest rates of home work participation among women with children aged fourteen to seventeen. Families in my study showed this same pattern, not an illogical association considering avowed concern for the care of their young children initially prompted their entry into home work. This cautions us to consider home work not as a lifelong oppressive pattern but as a potentially flexible one, depending on the resources available to the family. The circumstances under which women and men enter and leave home work to return to conventional employment as their children grow up should provide us with needed insight into this relationship. This study focused deliberately on intact families currently performing home work occupations but studies of families who have quit home work would enhance our understanding of the very complex interplay between characteristics of the home worker him/herself, nature of the specific job, and stage of family development.

Finally, this study scrutinized the life of home-working families with the intent of understanding and communicating their experiences. As such, it is a piece of work-family interaction research designed to explore how these two powerful social systems fit together, based on the family's perspective. I chose to examine families working at home because they offer one example of a range of potential opportunities for integrating work and family life, an example in which I thought all family members might play a role. I believe I have reported their perceptions accurately.

However, the experience of home-working families on a personal level does indeed connect with a larger economic context. Although I alluded to some elements of this context in chapter 2, other writers have focused more intensely on that level. Boris (1985, 1987) particularly describes the gender constructions which exploit and stigmatize home workers. Others, like Johnson (1982), focus on the exploitive nature of home work, especially among non-English speaking and/or illegal immigrants. Fernandez-Kelly and Garcia (1985) explore how the interrelationship among gender, politics, and economics created two different environments for home work among Cuban and Mexican women in Florida and California. Any contemporary researcher knows that race, class, and gender are significant variables affecting individual experiences; adding family as a variable further complicates the picture since present-day families come in a disparate array of structures and definitions. Thus, I would not argue that the experiences of these rural, white, intact home-working families represent the world of home-working families. What they do offer is a review of some crucial family variables which may affect the experience of home work as an integrative strategy, variables which may also affect families of other backgrounds, albeit in differing ways. What this and similar studies share is a deliberate focus on the family as an active agent, with the aim of uncovering points of divergence and convergence among families seeking to connect working and loving.

References

Abbott, E. 1910. *Women in industry.* New York: D. Appleton.

Andrisani, P. 1978. Job satisfaction among working women. *Signs, 3,* 588–607.

Becker, F. 1981. *Workspace: Creating environments in organizations.* New York: Praeger.

Benson, S. November 1979. *Women, work and the family economy.* Paper presented at the meeting of the Social Science History Association, Columbus, OH.

Best, F. 1978. Preferences on worklife scheduling and work-leisure tradeoffs. *Monthly Labor Review, 101;* (June), 31–37.

Blewett, M. 1983. Work, gender and the artisan tradition in New England shoemaking, 1780–1860. *Journal of Social History, 17,* 221–248.

Bloom-Feshbach, S., Bloom-Feshbach, J., and Heller, K. 1982. Work, family and children's perceptions of the world. In S. Kamerman and C. Hayes (Eds.), *Families that work: Children in a changing world* (pp. 268–307). Washington D.C.: National Academy Press.

Boneparth, E., and Stoper, E. 1983. Work, gender and technological innovation. In I. Diamond (Ed.), *Families, politics and public policy* (265–278). New York: Longman.

Boris, E. 1985. Regulating industrial homework: The triumph of "sacred motherhood." *Journal of American History, 71,* 745–763.

⎯⎯⎯ 1987. Homework and women's rights: The case of the Vermont knitters, 1980–1985. *Signs, 13,* 98–120.

Boulding, E. 1980. The labor of U.S. farm women—a knowledge gap. *Sociology of Work and Occupations, 7,* 261–290.

Branca, P. 1975. A new perspective on women's work: A comparative typology. *Journal of Social History, 9,* 129–153.

Bronfenbrenner, U. 1979. *The ecology of human development.* Cambridge: Harvard University Press.

Bronfenbrenner, U., and Crouter, A. 1982. Work and family through time and space. In S. Kamerman & C. Hayes (Eds.), *Families that work: Children in a changing world* (39–83). Washington D.C.: National Academy Press.

Chow, E., and Berheide, C. 1988. The interdependence of family and work: A framework for family life education, policy and practice. *Family Relations, 37,* 23–28.

Christensen, K. 1985. Women and home-based work. *Social Policy,* Winter, 54–57.

⎯⎯⎯ 1987. Women, families and home-based employment. In N. Gerstel and H. Gross (Eds.), *Families and work* (478–490). Philadelphia: Temple University Press.

Cott, N. 1977. **The bonds of womanhood. New Haven: Yale** University Press.

Degler, C. 1980. *At odds: Women and the family in America from the Revolution to the present.* New York: Oxford University Press.

diLeonardo, M. 1985. Women's work, work culture, and consciousness: An introduction. *Feminist Studies, 11,* 491–495.

Elman, M., and Gilbert, L. 1984. Coping strategies for role conflict in married professional women with children. *Family Relations, 33,* 317–327.

Faries, D. March 14, 1983. Home computers are nurturing working mothers. *San Jose Mercury News*, p. 2D.

Feldberg, R., and Glenn, E. 1982. Male and female: Job versus gender models in the sociology of work. In R. Kahn-Hut, A. Kaplan-Daniels, and R. Colvard (Eds.), *Women and work* (65–80). New York: Oxford University Press.

Fernandez-Kelly, M. Patricia, and Garcia, A. 1985. The making of an underground economy: Hispanic women, home work, and the advanced capitalist state. *Urban Anthropology, 14*, 59–90.

General Mills, Inc. 1981. *General Mills American family report 1980–81; Families at work: Strengths and strains.* Minneapolis: Author.

Gilligan, C. 1982. *In a different voice: Psychological theory and women's development.* Cambridge: Harvard University Press.

Glaser, B., and Strauss, A. 1967. *The discovery of grounded theory.* New York: Aldine.

Golden, S. 1975. Pre-school families and work. *Dissertation Abstracts International, 36,* 13979A. (University Microfilms No. 15347).

Gregg, G. April 13, 1986. Putting kids first. *New York Times Magazine,* pp. 47–51, 88, 97.

Guba, E. 1981. Criteria for assessing the trustworthiness of naturalistic inquiries. *Educational Communication and Technology Journal, 29,* (2), 75–91.

Hareven, T. 1975. The laborers of Manchester, New Hampshire, 1912–1922: The role of family and ethnicity in adjustment to family life. *Labor History,* (spring), 249–265.

———— 1982. *Family time and industrial time: The relationship between family and work in a New England industrial community.* New York: Cambridge University Press.

———— 1984. Themes in the historical development of the family. In R. Parke (Ed.), *Review of Child Development*

Research: Volume 7 (137–178). Chicago: University of Chicago Press.

Herbers, J. May 15, 1986. Cottage industries stir concern in U.S. *Portland Press Herald*, 34.

Herriott, R., and Firestone, W. 1983. Multisite qualitative policy research: Optimizing description and generalizability. *Educational Researcher, 12*, 2, 14–19.

Hewlett, S. 1986. *A lesser Life.* New York: William Morrow.

Hood, J., and Golden, S. 1979. Beating time/ making time: The impact of work scheduling of men's family roles. *Family Co-ordinator, 28*, 575–582.

Horvath, F. 1986. Work at home: new findings from the Current Population Survey. *Monthly Labor Review*, (November), 31–35.

How women view work, motherhood and feminism. March 31, 1986. *Newsweek,* 51.

Hunt, J., and Hunt, L. 1982. Dualities of careers and families: New integrations or new polarizations? *Social Problems, 29*, 499–510.

Jensen, J. 1980. Cloth, butter and boarders: Women's household production for the market. *Review of Radical Political Economics, 12* (2), 14–24.

Johnson, L. 1982. *The seam allowance.* Toronto: Women's Educational Press.

Kamerman, S. 1980. *Parenting in an unresponsive society.* New York: Free Press.

Kanter, R. 1977. *Work and family in the United States: A critical review and agenda for research and policy.* New York: Russell Sage Foundation.

Kantor, D., and Lehr, W. 1975. *Inside the family.* New York: Harper and Row.

Kessler-Harris, A. 1981. *Women have always worked.* Old Westbury, New York: Feminist Press.

Klagsbrun, F. 1985. *Married people: Staying together in the age of divorce.* New York: Bantam.

Klein, D.M., Jorgensen, S.R., and Miller, B.C. 1978. Research methods and developmental reciprocity in families. In R. Lerner and G. Spanier (eds.), *Child influences on marital and family interaction* (107–135). New York: Academic Press.

Kohn, M. 1977. *Class and conformity: A study in values with a reassessment.* Chicago: University of Chicago Press.

Kraut, R., and Grambsch, P. 1987. Home-based white collar employment: Lessons from the 1980 Census. *Social Forces, 66,* 410–426.

Lamphere, L. 1985. Bringing the family to work: women's culture on the shop floor. *Feminist Studies, 11,* 519–540.

Lasker, B. 1983. The emerging woman—integrating work and love. In M. Behr and W. Lazar (Eds.), *Women working home* (18–20). Edison, NJ: WWH Press.

Lein, L. 1974. *Final report: Work and family life* (National Institute of Education Project No. 3–3094). Cambridge: Center for the Study of Public Policy.

———— 1982. *Who does the housework? The allocation of work in the home as a reflection of family ideology.* (Working paper No. 92). Wellesley, Mass.: Wellesley College Center for Research on Women.

Matthei, J. 1982. *An economic history of women in America.* New York: Schocken Books.

McGaw, J. 1979. "A good place to work." Industrial workers and occupational choice: The case of Berkshire women. *Journal of Interdisciplinary History, 10,* 227–248.

Moore, W. 1973. Occupational socialization. In D. Goslin (Ed.), *Handbook of socialization theory and research* (861–883). Chicago: Rand McNally.

Noble, K. Aug. 20, 1986. U.S. weighs end to ban on factory homework. *New York Times,* p. A8.

Papenek, H. 1973. Men, women and work: Reflections on the two person career. *American Journal of Sociology, 78,* 857–872.

Piotrkowski, C. 1978. *Work and the family system.* New York: Free Press.

Pleck, E. 1976. Two worlds in one: Work and family. *Journal of Social History, 10,* 178–195.

Pleck, J. 1979. Men's family work: Three perspectives and some new data. *Family Co-ordinator, 28,* 481–488.

Pleck, J., and Lang, L. 1978. *Men's family role: Its nature and consequences.* Wellesley, Mass.: Wellesley College Center for Research on Women.

Porter, S. Jan. 5, 1983. Home industry evil is back. *Lewiston Daily Sun,* p. 9.

Presser, H. 1988. Shift work and child care among young dual earner American parents. *Journal of Marriage and the Family, 50,* 133–148.

Rapoport, R., and Rapoport, R. 1976. *Dual-career families re-examined.* New York: Harper.

Renshaw, J. 1976. An exploration of the dynamics of the overlapping worlds of work and family. *Family Process, 15,* 143–165.

Richardson, M. 1981. Occupational and family roles: A neglected intersection. *The Counseling Psychologist, 9* (4), 13–23.

Robinson, J. 1977. *How Americans use time: A social-psychological analysis of everyday behavior.* New York: Praeger.

Schulenberg, J., Vondracek, F., and Crouter, A. 1984. The influence of the family on vocational development. *Journal of Marriage and the Family, 46,* 129–143.

Shallcross, R. 1940. *Industrial homework.* New York: Industrial Affairs Publishing Company.

Staines, G., and Pleck, J. 1983. *The impact of work schedules on the family.* Ann Arbor: University of Michigan.

Stern, D., Smith, S., and Doolittle, F. 1975. How children used to work. *Law and Contemporary Problems, 39,* 93–111.

Taylor, A. Aug. 18, 1986. Why women managers are bailing out. *Fortune,* 16–23.

Teal, P. 1981. Women in the rural economy: Employment and self-employment. In S. Rosenfeld (Ed.), *Brake shoes, backhoes & balance sheets: The changing vocational education of rural women* (27–65). Washington D.C.: Rural American Women, Inc.

Thompson, E.P. 1967. Time, work-discipline and industrial capitalism. *Past and Present,* (December), 56–97.

Tilly, L., and Scott, J. 1978. *Women, work and family.* New York: Holt, Rinehart and Winston.

Toffler, A. 1980. *The third wave.* New York: William Morrow.

Trimberger, R., and MacLean, M. 1982. Maternal employment: The child's perspective. *Journal of Marriage and the Family, 44,* 469–475.

U.S. Department of Labor, Women's Bureau. 1935. *The commercialization of the home through industrial homework.* (Bulletin No. 135). Washington D.C.: Government Printing Office.

_____ 1935. *The employment of women in the sewing trades of Connecticut,* by C. Manning and H. Byrne. (Bulletin No. 109). Washington D.C.: Government Printing Office.

_____ 1935. *Industrial homework in Rhode Island, by H. Byrne and B. Blair. (Bulletin No. 131).* Washington D.C.: Government Printing Office.

_____ 1930. *Industrial home work,* by E. Brown. (Bulletin No. 79). Washington D.C.: Government Printing Office.

Vanek, J. 1980. Work, leisure and family roles: Farm households in the United States, 1920–1955. *Journal of Family History*, 5, 422–431.

Walker, A., and Thompson, L. 1984. Feminism and family studies. *Journal of Family Issues*, 5, 545–570.

Weitzman, L. 1985. *The divorce revolution: The unexpected social and economic consequences for women and children in America*. New York: Free Press.

Weller, L., and Luchterhand, E. 1969. Comparing interviews and observations on family functioning. *Journal of Marriage and the Family, 31*, 115–122.

Willmott, P., and Young, M. 1973. *The symmetrical family*. New York: Pantheon.

Index